REASON & BELIEF

REASON

&

**Problem Solving
in the
Philosophy of Religion**

BELIEF

TAMAL KRISHNA GOSWAMI

PUNDITS  PRESS

© 1997 Pundits Press
All rights reserved
Printed in the United States of America

First Edition

Pundits Press
5430 Gurley Avenue
Dallas, Texas 75223

ISBN 0-9643485-1-9
Library of Congress Catalog number: 97-067193

Contents

Acknowledgments

My indebtedness to my spiritual master His Divine Grace A.C. Bhaktivedanta Swami Prabhupada is endless. He taught me that reason divorced from belief is mental speculation while belief without reason can easily become fanaticism. These essays are a continuation of his conversation with western philosophy published in *Dialectic Spiritualism*. As one worships the Ganges by offering a palm full of her waters to her, may my spiritual master be pleased by this offering.

And may my academic mentor Dr. Lonnie Kliever be similarly satisfied that I have adequately represented his own philosophical tradition. He has patiently schooled me in the nuances of western thought, argued for its strengths, honestly revealed its flaws. His demand that I engage my own tradition with the same critical acumen he approaches his ensures the future of our ongoing dialogue. I thank him for his very gracious Introduction.

It is with great pleasure that I thank my dear brother Dr. Carl Herzig, Chairman of the English Department of St. Ambrose University, Iowa, for lending his expertise as an editor. Working together on this book has bound us closely in brotherly affection and common service and marks the start of what should prove to be a most fruitful reunion.

Mukunda Datta, Krishnavesha, and Radha Charan assisted with typing and research. Satyaraja gave the manuscript a final edit and offered helpful suggestions. Durashaya, Nitai Rama, Nitya Kishori, and Molly Hussing assisted in publishing, designing, and photography. Nrisinghadeva financed the project, while Dhananjaya provided services too numerous to list. Finally, I thank all of the devotees of our Dallas community who, like grown up children doting over their father, have enjoyed seeing me resume my studies, discontinued (as it turns out) for their sake some thirty years ago.

Introduction

Tamal Krishna Goswami first appeared at my office at Southern Methodist University in August of 1995. He was not a total stranger because a colleague and I had been his guests for lunch a year earlier. But he came with a strange request—he wanted to know what would be involved in pursuing a doctoral degree in Comparative Religions. He explained that he wanted to represent the tradition of Krishna Consciousness more effectively in interreligious dialogue and he believed that meant learning more about the religions of the world.

Goswami was obviously not prepared for the answer I gave him. Learning that he like many other students of the Sixties had dropped out of college in a quest for enlightenment, I advised him that he first would have to complete his undergraduate degree. I further explained that, unless he were prepared to complete an M.A. degree, he should major in Religious Studies. The heavens must have laughed at the irony—a fifty year-old ISKCON spiritual master returning to college as an undergraduate major in Religious Studies at a Methodist University! But Goswami was in no joking mood and he insisted that there must be some other way. He peppered me with questions: "What about life-time learning credit? What about testing out of courses?" In reply, I insisted that it was not the *degree* that he needed but the *training*. He could not hope to enter or complete a graduate program in Comparative Religions without a solid foundation in the methods and the content of the academic study of religion.

I thought that would be the end of my association with Tamal Krishna Goswami, but it was only the beginning. A few days later, I learned that he was ready to go forward in completing his undergraduate degree and that he wanted to begin in the fall.

Never mind that undergraduate admissions decisions are made in March! Never mind that none of his credentials were on hand! Doubtlessly remembering his early years as a missionary and builder of ISKCON when the word "impossible" did not exist, he was ready to get started yesterday. Fortunately, he had gained the interest of someone who knew the right people and how things work, and I was able to secure his admission to the University in the fall of 1995.

To say that he entered a strange world is an understatement. A man of recognized authority and deserved respect, he was suddenly one undergraduate among five thousand others. To be sure, he stood out from the crowd with his shaved head and ocher robes. But no quarter was given and none asked. As I told the group of his disciples celebrating the Appearance Day of their Beloved Spiritual Master last spring, Goswami does not sit on a velvet-cushioned *vyasasana* fanned by peacock feathers and ox-tails in his classes. Rather, he is crammed into uncomfortable chairs in crowded lecture halls like his fellow undergraduates. He is tested and tried in class discussions and written assignments like everyone else. But I also assured them that he was reaching more people through his vivid presence and stellar performance in classes at S.M.U. than he might ever reach in the sacred precincts of ISKCON temples.

Although we have talked often about the difficulties of his balancing two careers and living in two worlds, I can only guess at the energy and effort required for Goswami to maintain his spiritual calling and duties while pursuing his academic vision and studies. How does one live with integrity in such different worlds, demanding such different loyalties? What I do know is that he has given himself to the academic community with the same intensity and dedication that must characterize his service to his religious community. Some small measure of that devotion is seen in his 4.0 Grade Point Average and the academic awards he has accumulated in his two years at S.M.U. In 1996, he won the *1996 Harvey Paul Alper Award for Outstanding Work in an Eastern Religion*, and this year he received the *Isaac Gustave Bromberg Award for Outstanding Work in the Humanities* and the *Department of Religious Studies Annual Writing Award.* Even more impressive than these departmental awards, Goswami has made the Dean's List of Dedman College every semester, and this year was inducted into S.M.U.'s prestigious Robert Stewart Hyer Society and received the Society's *University Achievement Award.* Not satisfied with local academic achievements, Goswami also presented two scholarly papers at the 1996 National Meeting of the American Academy of Religion in New Orleans, the world's largest professional society of religion scholars with a membership nearing ten thousand. All this as an undergraduate major in Religious Studies!

This present collection of essays represents the fruit of only one undergraduate course among the seventeen that Goswami has completed to date. These essays were written for my introductory course on *Problems in the Philosophy of Religion.* All of my undergraduate courses are "writing-intensive," reflecting my own commitment to train students how to *think* philosophically rather than how to *memorize* information. In this class, every student was required to prepare ten papers based on assigned readings which called for a critical analysis and comparative response to the issues under discussion. The first nine essays were prepared as weekly assignments. The last longer essay was submitted as a take-home final examination.

Needless to say, Goswami's papers for this course were outstanding by every standard of judgment. His essays were written with grace and clarity. His discussion of the issues under review were models of fairness and accuracy. Best of all, his response to these issues from his own tradition were thoughtful and germane. Given where he is in his academic career, these essays showed a remarkable talent for interreligious dialogue—a talent for engaging questions of common concern between significantly different religious traditions. Going well beyond simple comparison or confession, these essays reflected a serious wrestle with philosophical ideas from divergent viewpoints which respects differences as well as searches out similarities.

Given their distinctive subject matter, Goswami and I talked about what to do with these essays. While interesting and informative in their own right, they were after all merely exploratory essays based on a single secondary source. As such, they did not represent finished scholarship—that is, they were not essays based on multiple primary sources offering detailed explorations and closely argued conclusions concerning the central problems in philosophy of religion. We seriously considered the possibility of his expanding and refining these essays based on wider reading in the primary source materials of the numerous philosophers discussed in the text. But with my encouragement, Goswami decided to publish these essays as they stand without further research and rewriting.

My reasons for lending my encouragement to the publication of these *student* essays are threefold. First, the core text is an up-to-date and sophisticated introduction to the philosophy of religion. Written by Michael Peterson, William Hasker, Bruce Reichenbach, and David Basinger, *Reason and Religious Belief: An Introduction to Philosophy of Religion* reflects the remarkable resurgence of interest in religion among professional philosophers of the last half century. It makes both classical and contemporary thinkers accessible, distilling and discussing the issues which the more complex and difficult primary literature engages. Thus, Goswami's chapter-by-chapter analyses of this text bring him into dialogue with the best thinkers on the whole range of problems in modern philosophy of religion.

Second, these ten essays are compelling evidence of the importance of Goswami's academic work for his faithful followers and godbrothers. More like field notes than finished documents, they nevertheless clearly map out a rich field of interreligious dialogue to be engaged and explored in the future. They indicate that ISKCON rests on a philosophical tradition that is every bit as sophisticated as classical and contemporary philosophical thinkers in western culture. They portend that ISKCON is prepared to participate in interreligious dialogue as full partners in scholarly debate over common questions and shared themes. As such, they should lend assurance to ISKCON's faithful that their tradition deserves the devotion of insiders and the respect of outsiders.

Finally, these ten essays should be of interest to curious or critical outsiders wanting to know more about ISKCON. They present an ISKCON community taking important steps to establish itself in the wider community of modern religions by entering into critical dialogue with those diverse traditions. They also provide hard-to-get information about how the Chaitanya Vaishnava tradition deals with such perennial philosophical issues as the nature of religious experience, the existence of God, the problem of evil, the peculiarity of religious language, the possibilities of miracle, the prospect of an afterlife, as well as how this tradition might respond to questions concerning religion and science, religious pluralism, and religious ethics.

Perhaps I may be indulged a personal reason for wanting to see these essays published in their present form. Goswami's work in my Philosophy of Religion class, as well as the half dozen other courses he has taken with me, are the kind of *gifts* that every teacher treasures. A student pays his teacher no greater honor than to discover his own voice in their common quest for knowledge. I hear such a voice emerging in these essays— thoughtful but passionate, critical but irenic, searching but secure. I would like for others to share in that gift and listen for that voice.

Lonnie D. Kliever
Professor and Chair
Department of Religious Studies
Southern Methodist University

CHAPTER 1

Religious Experiences

Religious experiences—encounters with the Divine—have shaped the course of religious history. Indeed, one could rightly ask if religion without such experience is even possible. What would Judaism be if Moses had not received the Law, or Christianity if none had believed in the resurrection? Islam without Mohammed's revelation? A non-enlightened Buddha? Hinduism minus *samadhi*? Surely, without such experiences, or at least the belief in them, human history would need to be rewritten.

The founders and followers of every major religion have rooted their beliefs and practices in the fertile soil of a transcendental plane where man contacts the Supreme and, as a result, is transformed. If these sacred moments have proven so foundational, what exactly is their nature? Is there a common, interfaith "core" to these experiences? Can they be trusted, and, if so, to what degree do they shape our faith in God?

A comprehensive classification of religious experiences has been suggested by Richard Swinburne based upon how the experiences take place. He lists five possibilities: they will be mediated either through a common, public, sensory object; through an unusual, public, sensory object; through a private object that can be described in normal sensory language, or one that can not; or finally, they will not be mediated by any sensory object at all (Peterson et al. 14-15). Swinburne's opinion is that these conditions are mutually exclusive. In any case, what is really important is to note their diversity, and to bear in mind the unique feature that distinguishes such events: they exert a special influence because they are taken to be supramundane, unlike the flux of life's ordinary happenings.

Granted the speciality of such experiences, how would they best be described? Are they emotional, perceptual, or supernatural? Each view has its convincing supporters, though their arguments are not beyond question. For example, Friedrich Schleiermacher, the father of modern theology, contended that faith is a self-authenticating "feeling of absolute or total dependence upon a source or power that is distinct from the world" (16). It is an intuitive rather than cognitive experience. Rudolf Otto, another supporter for the primacy of feeling or emotion, argued that God's deeper nature—his Holiness—cannot be grasped by reason. Feelings of dependence, awe, and longing are the subtle keys to the *sanctum sanctorum*, which cannot be unlocked by concepts and ideas, the tools of philosophy and theology. But then, if God is ineffable and the experience of him a non-cognitive act, how are the substantive aspects of religion, e.g. beliefs and practices, ever formulated? Furthermore, what is the proof that emotions are in fact divorced from concepts, beliefs, language, and a host of other factors? As simple and appealing as this view may seem, it raises some serious doubts.

A second view identifies religious experience as a type of perception. William Alston, a champion of this thesis, finds that perceptions, whether religious or ordinary, have similar elements: the perceiver, the perceived object, and the phenomenon (18). But, argue objectors, religious experiences are often non-sensory or are centered on a mediating object which differs significantly from God. It is therefore a mistake to regard such experiences as forms of perception similar to the perception of ordinary objects.

Alston counters this charge by demanding that a distinction

be made between an object's phenomenal and objective qualities. In ordinary perception we usually refer to the experienced object by using comparative concepts to describe how we would expect the object to look under normal conditions. Phenomenal qualities describing an object's precise appearance at a specific moment are rarely given. Similarly, we can use comparative concepts when reporting our experience of God's qualities, such as power, goodness, and love. Alston tells us, for example, that we can describe God's goodness by a comparison with human goodness. But this explanation does not satisfy his critics, who point out that information about humans is available through direct sense perception, and can be as precise as necessary. Visionary accounts of God are typically as vague as they are diverse.

Yes, agrees Wayne Proudfoot, there will be as many divergent accounts as there are belief systems. Debating in favor of a supernatural explanation for religious experience, he sets aside the thesis of perception by emphasizing belief in the experience itself rather than in the believable object. Whether or not the object exists is irrelevant; what counts is that one believes it does. Proudfoot terms this belief "supernatural" (21), because the believer will accept no other explanation for the event. He will reject any naturalistic cause and prefer to understand his experience in terms of his own belief system, which includes belief that the experienced object exists. This is a clear repudiation of Schleiermacher and Otto's view of an emotionally based experience devoid of prior concepts. But it also creates its own problems. Now each religious system becomes the judge of the veracity of its adherents' experiences. Objective, intrareligious evaluation becomes impossible.

Is there no "common core" to religious experience? Walter T. Stace is inclined to think there is. Concerned primarily with mystical experiences, Stace cites seven features a core mystical experience should include (23). But upon reading the first—that a mystic must experience the Void—one cannot help but wonder how such an interpretive postulation can be universally applied. Stace further damages his thesis by assigning different values to extrovertive and introvertive mysticism. Such evaluative judgments and restrictive definitions (e.g. "the Void") dim any hope of finding a common core.

Steven Katz swings the argument convincingly in that direction. Echoing Proudfoot, he asserts that all experiences are tied to concepts and beliefs: "'. . . these images, beliefs, symbols, and rituals define, *in advance*, what the experience *he wants to have*, and which he then does have, will be like'" (24). And what of the similar descriptions of religious encounters? They are only apparent, Katz says, for the often-vague terms have actual meanings unique to each encounter.

Katz's reasoning seems sound. He has been challenged that his view cannot account for some fundamental features of mystical experience. Perfection, or pure consciousness, it is claimed, is a state that transcends all categories and experiences, thus nullifying the very basis of Katz's contention. But this challenge, as much as Stace's definition of "the Void," is flawed by interpretation. Furthermore, categories like "higher-stage mystical states" are evaluative and therefore equally spurious. Is true perfection attained, as Katz's critics suggest, when "the yogi achieves pure consciousness, in which all categories, ideas, and external input are *forgotten*" (25)? A great sage's testimony of his experience of mystic perfection, from the *Bhagavata Purana* (Canto 1, Chapter 6, Texts 15-19) tells an entirely different story:

> After that, under the shadow of a banyan tree in an uninhabited forest I began to meditate upon the Supersoul situated within, using my intelligence, as I had learned from liberated souls. (15)

> As soon as I began to meditate upon the lotus feet of the Personality of Godhead with my mind transformed in transcendental love, tears rolled down my eyes, and without delay the Personality of Godhead Sri Krishna appeared on the lotus of my heart. (16)

O Vyasadeva, at that time, being exceedingly overpowered by feelings of happiness, every part of my body became separately enlivened. Being absorbed in an ocean of ecstasy, I could not see both myself and the Lord. (17)

The transcendental form of the Lord, as it is, satisfies the mind's desire and at once erases all mental incongruities. Upon losing that form, I suddenly got up, being perturbed, as is usual when one loses that which is desirable. (18)

I desired to see again that transcendental form of the Lord, but despite my attempts to concentrate upon the heart with eagerness to view the form again, I could not see Him any more, and thus dissatisfied, I was very much aggrieved. (19)

Perhaps the most striking feature of the sage Narada's narrative with regard to our immediate concern is that it demonstrates that in pure consciousness "all categories, ideas, and external input" need *not* be forgotten. But certainly all *mundane* ideas and externals are set aside by the appearance of his worshipful object of veneration.

Narada's experience seems to fall clearly within Swinburne's fifth possibility of experiencing God without any mediating object. It is a highly emotional experience ("tears rolled down my eyes"), full of feelings of dependence and longing, and one that Schleiermacher and Otto would approve. But it is not an ineffable, non-cognitive vision as they would expect. Narada clearly describes that he saw a transcendental form, specifically that of Sri Krishna. That the vision "erases all mental incongruities" does not imply a purely intuitive act without cognitive experience, because he states that he gained the vision lucidly, by "using his intelligence," and that it "satisfies the mind's desire." His mind as well as his senses remain fully activated, as the famous *Bhagavata* commentator A.C. Bhaktivedanta Swami Prabhupada explains in his purport to Text 17:

Spiritual feelings of happiness and intense ecstasies have no mundane comparison. Therefore it is very difficult to give expression to such feelings. We can just have a glimpse of such ecstasy in the words of Sri Narada Muni. Each and every part of the body or senses has its particular function. After seeing the Lord, all the senses become fully awakened to render service unto the Lord because in the liberated state the senses are fully efficient in serving the Lord. As such, in that transcendental ecstasy it so happened that the senses became separately enlivened to serve the Lord. This being so, Narada Muni lost himself in seeing both himself and the Lord simultaneously.

This final line should not be misunderstood as a loss of individuality through a merging with the Ultimate One, the monistic perfection most commonly ascribed to Eastern mysticism. This is classic theism: the servant *and* his worshipful Deity. While the perceiver and the perceived remain individual, there is a oneness of spirit which removes the pangs of material duality.

Narada's experience defies Alston's perceptual concepts because it is both phenomenal *and* objective. The perceived object, the Lord's form, has sensory qualities and does not require mediation. By stating that he sees Sri Krishna, he does far more than report comparative concepts, for if pressed he can provide relevant phenomenal details. Yet his description will closely resemble what other Krishna devotees behold, i.e., Krishna's objective qualities as defined by the religious system. This is in line with Proudfoot's view of the supernatural, and adheres to Katz's formula that prior beliefs and religious tradition shape one's religious experiences.

This is particularly relevant in Narada's case, for he practiced meditation according to previously received instructions and training which he "learned from liberated souls," a disciplic system explained by Peterson et al.:

> As confirmation of this position, note the role of gurus and teachers of the mystical tradition. The relevant wisdom is closely held by small

groups of devotees, led by a master or teacher who instructs them in a specific method for achieving the desired goal. Hence, the mystic experience itself is conditioned by the methods and beliefs instilled by the teacher. The attainment of genuine mystic insight is sanctioned, if not determined, by the master. (24)

The emphasis here on the role of the guru needs to be qualified. Gurus are not free to teach as they like. They draw from a 'depositorium of truth' which in this case includes not only the ancient Vedas, but the experiences of other accomplished yogis as well. It would be safe to say that Narada already had firm faith in the efficacy and goals of his meditation prior to his experience. Having already given his intellectual consent, he did not attempt the practice to test the validity of what he had learned. Vedic teaching, however, expects that every individual should make a personal endeavor for self-realization.[1] Narada's efforts and eventual encounter with God were a fulfillment of the teachings, naturally fortifying his faith.

But is Narada's success acceptable by those of different religious persuasions, or yet to others who would insist on natural causes? "One response is that we can evaluate the veracity of religious experience claims only within particular belief systems. That is, the explanation of the experience must be internally consistent with the set of beliefs and concepts that the experiencer uses" (22). Responding to the claim that this will not be a truly objective assessment, Peterson et al. refer to Swinburne's Principle of Credulity by saying, "We are justified in holding the belief until contrary considerations are introduced that would cast doubt upon either this particular perception or the accurate functioning of our perceptual apparatus in general" (28).

The Vedic meditational process ensures internal consistency by describing the deepening emotional changes the meditator will

---

[1] The term Vedic is used in its most broad sense to include not only the four Vedas and the *Upanishads* but all literature in pursuance of the Vedas; i.e., Smriti as well as Shruti.

experience as he makes incremental advancement. When Narada says that his "mind transformed in transcendental love," he uses the technical Sanskrit term *bhava-nirjita*. And when he becomes "exceedingly overpowered by feelings of happiness," the term *prema-atibhara* is used. These words, as well as other descriptions of his symptoms, inform a knowledgeable person that Narada's advancement is of the highest degree.

Yet even if internal consistency can be demonstrated, those of scientific bent (whether of the social or the natural sciences) will hardly be satisfied. They will try to attribute Narada's experience to natural causes. And because repeatability and predictability are essential elements of the experimental test, they will certainly want to understand why his practice did not yield the same results a second time. The only answer to this is that "religious experience cannot be reduced to any other kind of experience . . . [It] requires the supernatural explanation as part of its description" (21). The purport by Bhaktivedanta Swami Prabhupada to Text 19 makes this explicit:

> There is no mechanical process to see the form of the Lord. It completely depends on the causeless mercy of the Lord. We cannot demand the Lord to be present before our vision, just as we cannot demand the sun to rise whenever we like. The sun rises out of his own accord; so also the Lord is pleased to be present out of His causeless mercy. One should simply await the opportune moment and go on discharging his prescribed duty in devotional service of the Lord. Narada Muni thought that the Lord could be seen again by the same mechanical process which was successful in the first attempt, but in spite of his utmost endeavor he could not make the second attempt successful. The Lord is completely independent of all obligations. He can simply be bound up by the tie of unalloyed devotion. Nor is He visible or perceivable by our material senses. When He pleases, being satisfied with the sincere attempt of devotional service depending completely on the mercy of the Lord, then He may be seen out of His own accord.

We may have to accept the fact, as William James states, that certain questions—like "Is there God?"—can never be settled by experimental or logical tests, but only in the 'laboratory of human experience.' Human individuality ensures that each human experience be unique, just as common themes insure their creditability. Religious experiences, however, being uncommon, are usually viewed with suspicion. But rarity alone is not a just grounds for rejection. As Peterson et al. state, "Consonance with other justified beliefs about God and religious practices might be one way to winnow out less reliable claims" (28).

One thing is certain: to reject religious experiences wholesale would be an untenable thought. It would bring down the curtain of religious history and shroud the world under the dark mantle of secularism. Encounters with the Divine are a beacon of light, and not only for a fortunate few. Hearing of such experiences provides the faithful with a vision of God, and, of equal importance, illuminates their earthly path of morality, and gives hope that they too may one day attain that divine vision.

CHAPTER 2

Theistic Arguments

Since the dawn of human life—whether in Eden or on the primate ladder—there has been belief in a supernatural power. Whether it be the stern voice of the Lord God or a lightning bolt from above, Adam or the primitive were forced to believe in someone or something of vast superiority. Time has not substantially changed this basic belief passed on through human history like an inherited trait. But having eaten of the tree of the knowledge of good and evil, we no longer stand naked in body or in thought. Clothed in doubts, we now demand to know *why* we should believe. We demand evidence and proof more than voices and bolts of lightning. Without reason and logic it is doubtful our faith can survive. But can our belief in God be subjected to such rational tests? Are the methods of science and philosophy equally applicable in the study of religion?

First we must establish that the proof of God's existence is truly essential. It is, certainly, for those who believe that God plays an essential role in their life and destiny. And it is no less important to those who feel otherwise and are seeking reasons to justify their position. Considering such opposed views, it is most unlikely that even the best-argued proof for or against God's existence will satisfy everyone, prejudiced as people are by their prior convictions. Better that we adopt a "person-relative" view of proof, and consider community acceptance a secondary merit.

This in mind, what are the characteristics that elevate irrational beliefs to the realm of "proofs" (69)? First, arguments must be sound, which means that conclusions must logically follow valid premises. Second, a proof is an argument that someone, but not necessarily everyone, *knows* to be sound. Third, proofs must "extend our knowledge"; the premises should be more readily knowable than the conclusion and should not be based on the conclusion itself. If it be objected that every premise supporting the existence of God first be proven, an infinite series of arguments would need to be constructed. Not only would this violate our third principle by forcing each premise to be inferred from its conclusion, but it is a task that would defy any finite human.

Enough said; accepting the above criteria, let us test some of the most outstanding arguments to see if they establish God's actuality. We shall survey the teleological and moral arguments in particular, setting aside for another time those which are ontological and cosmological. Finally, we shall assess some reasonings postulated by the Vaishnava theistic tradition of India.

Teleology, the philosophical study of evidence of design in nature, marshals together seemingly ordinary facts to establish the extraordinary case for God's being. To demonstrate the intricate "means-ends adaptation" that exists in nature, William Paley chose the analogy of a simple watch (80). Its tiny gears, wheels, and springs which together keep perfect time did not arise and assemble themselves spontaneously. Just so, all the parts of the eye and the end of seeing, or for that matter any aspect of nature, present the same means-ends adaptation. Since the effects in the watch and nature are analogous, they must share an analogous cause: an intelligent, purposeful maker.

The analogy was not so obvious to David Hume. Anticipating Paley's argument, he forwarded three compelling reasons to refute it (80). If an analogy depends on points of similarity, mechanical watches and organic nature are worlds apart. Secondly, Hume argued, though reason may govern man-made creations, there are other principles at work in nature; generation, vegetation, and gravity each rule particular domains. It is incorrect to transpose one paradigm onto another. Finally, once the principle of causality is summoned to explain the existence of God, then God must answer to that same summons. Such a demand will lead to the fault of infinite regress. Therefore, either we deny causation altogether or else allow that both matter and God are legitimate disputants in the claim for primacy.

This last alternative was particularly attractive to evolutionary naturalists, who considered natural selection and survival of the fittest a suitable explanation for the means-end order of nature. As far as they were concerned, God was now peacefully at rest in his grave.

"Nonsense!" the theists quickly retort. They have mounted an impressive defense by arming their teleological arguments with contemporary examples inductively reasoned. They grant that evolution can *describe* means-end ordering to some extent, but find that it cannot actually *explain* it (81). In this sense it is a rather "trivial" or "circular" principle. One would expect a scientific explanation to follow the hypothetical-deductive method, but the theory of natural selection is unable to predict specific outcomes from the theory and then test that they follow. Evolutionists admit that biology is not as predictable as physics or other sciences and suggest that its role as an interpretive paradigm is sufficient. However, this reply, as Peterson et al. correctly state, leaves "the door ajar" (82); it simply plays into the hands of the inductive teleological theists, providing them enough room to enter and stockpile their accumulated evidence which they are certain will prove their hypothesis to be the most reasonable.

Natural selection, it is first pointed out, cannot explain certain aspects of the universe. It cannot, for example, explain why non-living elements should give rise to life rather than to the non-living. Or how so many disparate conditions—e.g., the expansion rate and the physical-chemical composition of the universe; the distance of the earth from the sun; the ratio of the masses of the proton and electron—are so ideally arranged to support life. Whatever explanations are offered are of such low probability compared to "[t]he appeal to a conscious, purposive designer [which] better explains the life-anticipating conjunction of these extremely narrowly ranged physical conditions and natural laws" (83).

Natural selection also cannot account for the fact that organisms develop towards greater complexity, for complexity is not always necessary for survival of the fittest. Furthermore, sophisticated information processing occurs at the microbiological level, such as the information-ordered nucleotides of the double helix. Where does the information come from? And which came first—such information, or someone to read it? In natural selection, both would have to arise simultaneously to ensure that either was useful, and hence, selected.

The inductive teleological theists conclude their arguments with the accusation that natural selection inadequately explains how the various aspects and laws of nature result in an all-pervasive order that is so mathematically precise that it can be used to predict the future. Natural selection is *so* inadequate, they challenge, it cannot even explain itself!

And what of inductive teleology? "In sum, the inductive teleological argument asks not who made the amoebae or the elephant, but how one accounts for the entire system that, developing from the simple to the complex, from the nonliving to the living, portends conscious life" (84). Building upon ordinary facts, the sheer weight of evidence from unrelated areas of science leads one to conclude that a governing, life-anticipating order is the design of a supremely intelligent being.

This conclusion is amplified by philosophers like Immanuel Kant, and more recently by C.S. Lewis, postulators of the moral argument (85). Their contention is that our very sense of morality, visible in our discussions and behavior, tells of an *objective moral* law that can be understood rationally. They reject moral relativism because without a yardstick to measure by, there would be no criterion to judge right from wrong. Nor would there be any inducement for moral progress. Advocates of moral relativism suggest that their position allows for greater tolerance and accommodation, but this in itself constitutes a moral judgment on their part, namely that tolerance is preferable to intolerance. Finally, if it be argued that different societies have varying standards of morality, Lewis replies that there is actually substantial agreement amongst them about what is morally acceptable and what is forbidden.

Lewis next seeks the cause for objective moral law. He suggests two possibilities: the factual reality of human experience (which he calls "matter") and mind. But reality describes only what happens, not what *ought* to happen. Free will, in other words, differentiates moral law from the laws of nature, which are mandatory. Behind all of these laws is a law maker, as Lewis states, "'urging me to do the right and making me feel responsible and uncomfortable when I do wrong. I think we have to assume it is more like a mind than it is like anything else we know—because after all the only thing we know is matter and you can hardly imagine a bit of matter giving instructions'" (86).

Naturalistic ethicticians like Aristotle may explain that moral directives, like all else, should follow the pattern of an ordered and harmonious universe. But this argument, though materialistic, does not preclude the possibility of a "pattern maker." It is that same universe maker, the moral argument goes, who makes objective moral laws as well. The moral argument does more than merely support the teleological conclusion. Because its jurisdiction includes the social obligations among humans themselves and as well as those to God, it swings the theistic argument clearly in the direction of a supreme personality of Godhead.

To be certain, the personal, loving God worthy of worship has not yet emerged in this line of reasoning. The above teleological and moral arguments present a distinctively philosophical being, one that would hardly content religionists. There is, however, the possibility of a healthy correlation, and it is this which we will now examine in the light of the Vaishnava theistic doctrines and their oral tradition as expounded by their foremost modern proponent, A.C. Bhaktivedanta Swami Prabhupada.

Before beginning, let us refer back to our original definition of a person-relative proof as a proof that should be sound at least in reference to that person in question, and whose premises hold true even without being inferred from the conclusion. The Vaishnava—and in a larger context all those who use the Vedic system of reasoning—will have trouble with this definition. Following the standard approach of systematic theology, Vaishnavas will accept as normative their sources of truth, namely, the Vedic scriptures. They will be hesitant to accept as truth that which may be flawed by human defect. These human defects include the commission of errors, the possibility of becoming illusioned, the propensity for cheating, and sensual imperfection. Vedic thinkers consider *pratyaksha* (direct evidence) and *anumana* (inductive reasoning) secondary to *shabda* (Vedic assertion). By direct evidence the sun appears no larger than a small disk, but it is actually far larger than many planets. Therefore, *pratyaksha* is imperfect. Induction makes use of hypotheses, which implies uncertainty. Darwin, for example, made extensive use of induction to reach his conclusions which, despite their wide acceptance, are still labeled as "theory." Because of the potential for human error, these two methods are used only to support *shabda*, which is considered divinely derived. This having been said, we may now proceed to examine some arguments for the existence of

God, and others which discount his existence.

The Christian theologian Anselm has proposed a concept of God as "a being than which none greater can be conceived" (70). This will naturally entail a description of such a being's characteristics. The great Vedic authority Parashara Muni has stipulated that the supreme being should possess six qualities: all wealth, all strength, all fame, all beauty, all knowledge, and all renunciation. According to the *Vishnu Purana* (6.5.74), when these kinds of opulence are present in someone to a superlative degree, that person is *Bhagavan* (God) (qtd. in *Kanthahara* 99-100). This is also stated in the Vedic literature as *"asama urdhva,"* which means that no one is found equal to him or greater than him.

The kalam cosmological argument that there must exist some necessary being, refers to cause or personal agent. The same is expressed by Lord Krishna in the *Bhagavad-gita* (14:4): "It should be understood that all species of life, O son of Kunti, are made possible by birth in this material nature, and that I am the seed-giving father."

As A.C. Bhaktivedanta Swami Prabhupada once explained:

> Just as everyone has father, all living entities are coming originally from this original father. The father is there. Fact is fact, but anyone perceives it or not. You may not have seen my father, but you know that I had a father. You do not have to perceive him directly to know that he is a fact. Because I exist, my father is essential. That is understood and assumed by everyone. Therefore people say, "What is your father's name?" instead of, "Do you have a father?" It is assumed that one has a father, even though this father is not immediately perceived. (*Dialectic Spiritualism* 353)

The naturalists study how one species arise from another. They declare that "The order in the universe is not the product of conscious activity, but the result of natural selection, the prime mechanism of evolution" (Peterson et al. 81). The Vaishnavas assert that God is the prime-mover of the universe. Again from *Bhagavad-gita* (9:10): "This material nature is working under My direction, O son of Kunti, and it is producing all moving and non-moving beings. By its rule this manifestation is created and annihilated again and again." As Prabhupada says:

> The Pacific Ocean is calm and quiet. But when the superior force, air, pushes it, it manifests high waves. The ocean has no power to move without the superior force of the air. Similarly, there is another force superior to the air, and another and another, until ultimately we arrive at Krishna . . . Krishna controls nature such as an engineer controls a train. The engineer controls the locomotive, which pulls one car, and that car in turn pulls another, which pulls another, and so the whole train is moving. Similarly, with the creation, Krishna gives the first push, and then, by means of successive pushes, the entire cosmic manifestation comes into being and is maintained. (*Science* 219)

Denial of an absolute authority brings with it denial of accountability to such authority and causes one to question whether *any* levels of authority, standards of conduct, or codes of morality need be recognized. If the base pursuit of personal gratification becomes a person's sole motivation in life, then the result is a degeneration in moral behavior evident in such common place practices as abortion, drug abuse, and divorce. This parallels Lewis's objection to moral relativism. His "mind behind the universe" is a little vague, but nonetheless suggests something akin to the Vedic concept of *paramatma*, the form of God within the heart of all living beings who supplies conscience and discrimination. As Krishna asserts in the *Gita* (15:15): "I am seated in everyone's heart, and from Me comes remembrance, knowledge and forgetfulness."

Modern science claims that the favorable combination of material chemicals is responsible for life; a living and a dead body differ only in chemical composition. Prabhupada, while walking through the countryside one morning, pointed to a dead tree and remarked, "To prove their theory, they must be able to inject the proper chemicals and make branches and leaves grow again. The scientific process includes observation, hypotheses and then demonstration. . . . but the scientist cannot actually prove that life comes from matter; they simply make observations, hypotheses, but no demonstrations" (*Life* 11).

In all cultures of the world, even those considered primitive, some form of worship of God has always been extant. Scoffing at emotional "sentimentalists," atheists may dismiss this as simply a "psychological need," without questioning its ultimate cause or function. This innate desire in the human psyche to worship a supreme person speaks for the reality of God's existence as much as the craving to eat is indicative of the real need of the body for sustenance, or as the quest for knowledge is indicative of advanced intellectual functions.

Theists are frequently challenged to explain why God cannot be *seen*. The absence of any empirical proof strengthens such doubts. Prabhupada responds with characteristic humor: "People challenge, 'can you show me God?' but what can they see? They cannot even see their next-door neighbor. What is the value of their eyes? God is not cheap" (*Easy Journey* 54). When asked on another occasion if he had seen God, Prabhupada responded:

> Yes. God can be seen at every moment. Krishna says [in the *Gita*], "I am the taste of water." We drink water everyday, and the taste of water is there, so if we think of this taste as Krishna, we will have began realizing God everyday. Krishna further says, "I am the light of the sun and moon." Everyday we receive sunlight, and in the evening there is moonshine, so if we think of the source of these emanations, we will automatically become God conscious. (*Science* 302)

Certainly this is not an empirical proof in the usual sense, but we have already rejected this strong definition of proof in favor of a person-relative view. Prabhupada's statement should be understood in that light.

Some may argue that the concept of God is a figment of human imagination. Others contend that belief in God is a sign of weakness, a debilitating dependency, Marx's "opiate of the masses," but the lives of saintly persons from every tradition are testimony against such a claim. Service to God requires the utmost degree of conviction, courage, inspiration and strength, for to serve God often means to go against all established norms. To persevere in the face of such opposition is not the task of an emotionally dependent weakling. And, contrary to Marx's assessment, such saintly persons have often proven to be great social reformers as well.

But if God exists, others demand, why is there so much evil in the world? Here, God's own morality is being questioned. And a further doubt is also raised: How can an all-knowing God allow those who are good to suffer?

Prabhupada gave the following response when questioned about evil, using the analogy of a person to describe the material world:

> Unless there is evil, why are you in this material world? You have accepted evil; therefore you are in this material world. And if you accept God, the good, then you are in the spiritual world. But you don't accept God; you want evil. Therefore you are in the material world. Just like in jail. Who is in the prison house? Only criminals. Similarly, everyone of us who are within this material world are all criminals because we have disobeyed the orders of God. We are in different statuses only, but all criminals. Because everyone of us is subjected to the rules of nature: birth, death, old age, and disease. (*Conversations* vol. 13, 7).

Evil and suffering are explained by the concept of karma. According to the law of karma, the eternal spirit enjoys and suffers the reactions to every action at some point in the future through the agency of the subtle body—the mind, intelligence and false ego, or materially conditioned sense of identity. This subtle body, infected with material desires, binds the soul to a succession of reincarnations in the material world. It also impels the soul to act and become entangled hopelessly in the perplexities of karmic reaction. But the purpose of this process is actually the ultimate rectification of the spirit itself. A suffering person may inquire about the goal of life and how to become free from the suffering condition once and for all. Knowledge of one's constitutional position leads to detachment, a prerequisite for spiritual advancement. By adopting purifying practices, the devoted soul ultimately receives the merciful direction of the Lord within the heart, the ultimate giver of liberation from material existence.

God not only the makes the law of karma but gives the conditioned soul the free will to follow or disobey it. The sufferings undergone by the materially conditioned souls are actually their own doing, the result of their choice to ignore God. God sanctions this suffering with love as a responsible and concerned father, offering good guidance and counseling from within as the Supersoul, and without in the form of saintly persons and scripture. God never abandons the wayward soul, no matter how far the soul may stray. God is always all-good.

Let us end our discussion on theistic arguments by citing Peterson et al., whose concluding statement we fully embrace:

> Whatever one concludes about the relation between the Ultimate Being of the theistic arguments and the God of religion, it is important to note that what is at stake is not a conflict or correlation between two gods, but between two concepts of god. When seen from this perspective, the work of philosophers and that of theologians complement each other. The cumulative case of natural theology provides grounds for thinking that belief in God is reasonable, whereas the theologian puts this belief in a larger, salvational, revelational context. (88)

Philosophers and theologians, strange bedfellows as they may at times seem, may dwell comfortably in the same house. For, in their search for the Truth they have much in common, as had the primitives and Adam eons ago.

CHAPTER 3

The Problem of Evil

Christians often muse how different it would now be had Adam and Eve not tasted fruit from the tree of the knowledge of good and evil. Had they not succumbed to this temptation, they could have dwelled perhaps forever in that idyllic Garden of Eden created for them by the Lord God. Alas, such thoughts are no more than wishful thinking. Neither Adam and Eve, nor it seems, anyone since them has been able to exercise such stringent self-restraint, or avoid suffering the consequences. Who is to be blamed? Should we fault Eve alone, or Adam as well? Or, does every individual who subsequently erred bear responsibility? Or perhaps we should accuse the serpent? Certainly this third option is most tempting, because it frees us of personal guilt. But beware of temptation! Behind this serpentine allurement lies a deadly trap which may severely test our faith. For if we blame the serpent we may as well blame the serpent's master. And having gone so far, we may as well ask why an all-knowing and all-loving God made such a crafty creature at all. With full knowledge of human foibles, why did God set in motion such a doomed cause-and-effect situation which has led today to such suffering, inequality and injustice, disaster and death, to the human hurt and wickedness that pervades our world? To continue such questioning may even lead one to doubt the very existence of God. Yet human reason impels those thirsting for the truth to seek answers to these questions. Those who take such risk may find the tender creepers of their devotion strengthened by the ordeal that reason demands.

Any precise definition of evil will tend to favor one particular theory of evil over another. To avoid such prejudice, we may specify two broad categories of evil: *moral* evil and *natural* evil (93). Moral evil includes the wrongful acts and bad character traits of free human beings, while natural evil covers the physical pain and suffering resulting from either impersonal forces or human actions. With these commonsense notions in mind, we can compare and contrast the *logical* and *evidential* problems of evil.

Critics of theism, such as John Mackie, have underscored what they consider to be a basic inconsistency in believing, on the one hand, that an omnipotent, omniscient, perfectly good God exists, while on the other hand, admitting the existence of evil (94). For Mackie, the problem is not that religious beliefs lack rational support, or even whether or not they are true or false; he is concerned by the apparent illogic of simultaneously asserting two conflicting propositions. If God is all-capable, and if evil is unwanted, then evil should not exist.

This nontheistic assertion of inconsistency has been most strongly rebutted by Alvin Plantinga's Free Will Defense. Plantinga wishes to demonstrate the consistency of the two propositions by finding a third statement that is consistent with the first, and in conjunction with it, implies the second (95). The statement need only be possible, because determining consistency depends upon demonstrating the logic that exists between the statements, not necessarily the truth of any one or all of them. The third statement Plantinga has selected hinges on God's creating creatures with the freedom to choose moral good. This freedom allows creatures to choose evil as well. Thus, it is not within God's power to create a world containing moral good but no moral evil. This is Plantinga's third statement which, along with the assertion that God exists, implies that evil also exists.

Mackie and Antony Flew have challenged Plantinga by asking why a God who is all-powerful could not have created a world containing free creatures who *always* abide by moral good. Plantinga responds by insisting that God not be subjected to illogical expectations. As God cannot bring about married bachelors or square circles, neither can he create a world of free creatures who *always* act morally. Having given creatures that freedom, it is *their* prerogative, not God's. Plantinga's detractors, however, are not easily satisfied. They argue that free will and determinism are compatible—God could create a world in which all persons could have chosen to perform moral actions, although all of their choices were determined. Plantinga seems to put this compatibilist argument neatly to rest with the following precise definition of *significant freedom*: "'A person is free with respect to an action *A* at a time *t* only if no causal laws and antecedent conditions determine either that he performs *A* at *t* or that he refrains from so doing'" (97). This Free Will Defense, with its *incompatibilist* view, appears overall to be a strong response to the logical problem of evil.

While Plantinga has curtailed the compatibilist view, critics have made issue over the *evidential* form of the problem of evil. These critics are not as concerned with theistic inconsistency as much as they are with its *implausibility*. For them, the problem is not one of illogic but more a question of whether theism provides a reasonable explanation of what appears to be the fact of evil. Wesley Salmon is one of the most articulate of such critics. Given that evil does exist in the world, Salmon argues that the statement that "'An omnipotent, omniscient, perfectly good God does not exist'" has a much higher numerical probability than the statement "'An omnipotent, omniscient, perfectly good God exists'" (114).

Objections to Salmon's reasoning have been raised by

Plantinga as well as Nancy Cartwright. Salmon used mechanically created entities as a reference point for his proposition, since it was obviously impossible for him (or for that matter anyone) to assess the situation of evil that exists in *all* divinely created universes. But by doing so he begs the question in advance, as Cartwright correctly observes, comparing our universe with a mechanical model and thus insinuating that the universe has no divine origin (98). Cartwright argues further that statistical techniques are totally inappropriate when assessing metaphysical issues such as the existence of God. Plantinga's objections are along similar lines. Modern probability studies, he points out, are troubled by assigning probability to one statement on the basis of another without any clear criterion. The method of presenting statistical information can also be prejudiced if critics have a wholly natural world view.

A number of critics have voiced what is perhaps the strongest objection based on evidence: granted that a reasonable amount of evil may exist, how are we to explain evils that appear utterly pointless or gratuitous? If an omniscient, all-powerful, loving and reasonable God truly exists, certainly he would not allow for *pointless* evil. Defenders of theism counter that no matter how severe the evil may seem, there is a purpose and even ultimate benefit from it.

Rather than allowing this argument to reach a deadlock, which would obviously favor the critics, some theists have been willing to concede that God may indeed allow for gratuitous evil. They contend that God's granting humanity free will includes the risk of pointless evil. Theists hope that this accommodation will weaken the evidential argument.[1]

Plantinga and others have attempted to defend theism against

---

[1] This writer would suggest that such an accommodation may easily leave the theistic deity open to severe criticism unless we are reminded that accommodation does not imply *approval*. Every theistic tradition could cite numerous instances of the deity attempting to prevent such evil occurrences.

the charge of inconsistency or improbability. But a *defense* is not the same as providing a true and reasonable explanation for why God actually allows evil. A *theodicy* is "a systematic account of how various theistic beliefs about God and the moral venture shed light on evil in the world" (100). Theodicists have traditionally held to the classical theistic view of God in order to address the problem of evil.

One basic approach is to affirm that evil is a *necessary* contrast to the good; without evil we would have no way of assessing what is true goodness (103). An obvious response to this proposal is to question whether a much smaller dose of evil would not suffice to teach the same lesson. A second suggestion is that evil is God's *punishment* for the sinful. As he rewards righteousness, so he condemns wrongful acts. Well enough, critics reply, but how may we explain the wholesale destruction of entire populations or the death of an innocent infant?

Thinkers like Leibniz have postulated yet another view, that God deeply considered the value of evil before creating the *best of all possible worlds*, finding certain goods to outweigh their corresponding evils (104). Critics have assailed Leibniz on a number of accounts. First, the statement "best of all possible worlds" may be logically incoherent. How do we know that what we have is that best of all possible worlds? Second, ordinary moral judgment dictates that we always strive to improve our world; the Leibnizian proposal appears to deny this possibility. And third, why did God bother to create a world at all if this is the best that he could do?

Yet another treatment of the problem of evil is the *ultimate harmony* solution, which has two distinct approaches: that *all is well with the world from God's perspective*, or that *all will be well in the long run* (104-5). The supporters of this first approach theorize that only an infinite, wise God can comprehend and see ultimate good in the totality of good and evil events, whereas we finite beings cannot. This approach is assailable on two accounts:

(a) It frustrates human moral judgment, and (b) If the traditional Christian concept that humans are made in God's image holds true, then it should also follow that humans are capable of reasonable moral judgments.

A variant of the all's-well position is that since God's morality is so much higher than ours we necessarily are unable to apply the same perfect moral judgment in evaluating events as God would. Again, the weakness of this position is that it undercuts human moral judgment, and furthermore, since God's morality is so much higher than ours, how could we ever understand it, let alone use it to solve the riddle of evil? As J. S. Mill rightly concludes, to accept the higher-divine-morality approach one might as well abandon reason altogether.

Advocates of the other division of ultimate harmony, those of the all's-well-that-ends-well persuasion, claim that all evils will ultimately end in higher goods in the future, whether in this world or in the next. This viewpoint is open to similar attacks as those made against the all's-well-in-God's-sight position. But there are some specific criticisms as well. For example, how can we accurately evaluate whether future welfare *justifies* the present occurrence of related evils? "It is quite a conceptual jump from the notion of a good *outweighing* an evil to the notion of *compensating* for an evil, and a very large jump to the notion of a good *justifying* the existence of an evil" (106). Defenders of this view fall back on the pat response that we limited humans will never be able to fully understand what God's unlimited wisdom does.

Many of the previous solutions address moral evil, but there is one important solution that specifically addresses the problem of natural evil. This *natural law* explanation states that God created a world that works according to a certain predictable natural ordering, one that supports a moral order in which free choice allows humans to make intelligent deliberations. But this natural system also allows for natural evil. Critics like H. J.

McCloskey have argued that God could just as well reduce or eliminate all such natural evils by miraculous intervention or by creating a much-improved alternative natural system (106). Swinburne has effectively countered by reminding such critics that a natural order implies that God should not have to intervene often. On the whole, God has created a good and natural system that does not require the need of adjustment from outside.

As the above philosophy specifically explains natural evil, so the *free will* theodicy is especially meant to address the problem of moral evil. While Plantinga's Free Will Defense states merely that it is possible that God created creatures with free will, Free Will Theodicy states that God did indeed create morally free beings, knowing fully well that they would sometimes err, but nevertheless considering the investment of such freedom far more beneficial than if humans were to be mere mindless puppets. As could be guessed, critics again question the incompatibilist assumptions, much as they did those of the Free Will Defense. And those critics who are willing to overlook this point still argue that God could have created free human beings with a stronger tendency to do right than wrong. Theists typically respond that God has created humans with the maximum rightness without altogether eliminating freedom of choice.

In addition to the above theodicies, certain responses to the problem of evil have incorporated a broader vision of the origin and destiny of humanity and are therefore called *global theodicies*. Peterson et al. have described three of these: *Augustinian theodicy, Irenaean theodicy,* and *process theodicy* (107).

For St. Augustine, the whole of God's creation is good. Evil has no substantial existence independent of God, but is simply the absence of such goodness. Because the creation is mutable, goodness can be corrupted. It is the misuse of free will that allows the entry of sin or evil into human experience. This began with Adam's transgression, bringing guilt and punishment upon the whole race. But believers can be redeemed by divine grace, leading ultimately to the establishment of God's kingdom.

The elements of Augustinian theodicy have pervaded Christian thinking to the present day, supplying much of the theistic defense for the coexistence of God and evil. But fifteen hundred years have provided ample time for critics to carefully scrutinize Augustine's view. They charge that in light of God's supreme majesty and sovereignty, evil could easily be liquidated. Still more serious is the question of how originally pure creatures such as Adam and Eve could have chosen to do evil.

The pre-Augustian Bishop Irenaeus offered a theodicy that modern-day proponents like John Hick still advocate (108). Irenaean theodicy explains that Adam and the original creation were not perfect; instead, they were innocent but immature. Humans are meant to mature by experiencing temptation and gradually overcoming evil. Maturing implies growth, an impossible conception were God to have created morally perfect beings from the start.

Hick labels this "soul-making" theodicy, and states that in the face of real challenges, there is always the risk of evil—of failure and ruin, suffering and injustice. He even states that it is important that the world appear as if there is no God. Ultimately, God lends his helping hand, leading to the final result of universal salvation. Critics of Hick like G. Stanley Kane argue that such great challenges—severe moral and physical evils—are not required to induce faith nor to conceal God (109). The same could have been accomplished with much less pain. Neither does empirical evidence substantiate Hick's claim of soul-making. The endless list of human failings seems enough to bury his theory. And again, even if there were sufficient successes, are these enough to justify the degree of hardship and suffering required for their success? Hick seeks to skirt this last charge by granting each human the right to decide whether the price of salvation is worth it.

Certain philosophers, while rejecting the approach of non-theistic critics, have found the range of theodicies so dissatisfying that they have formulated what has come to be known as *process philosophy*. Persons like Alfred North Whitehead and Charles Hartshorne have rethought in striking ways the relationship between God and the world, emphasizing change, development, and evolution—not only in finite creatures but in God as well. God has two aspects: his primordial nature which contains all eternal possibilities for how this world may advance, and his consequent nature which contains the experiences and responses of creatures to the possibilities of how they may act in this world. As God's nature responds to such changes, he is said to change or be in process.

This is certainly a radical departure from traditional theistic belief. No longer do we have the divinely omnipotent, infinite Godhead. The 'traditional' God of old now *shares* his power. The 'process' God is powerful, but not all-powerful; creatures, too, have power of their own which makes their decisions truly free. The process God is *persuasive* rather than *coercive*, and, as David Griffin states, cannot single-handedly eliminate evil because he "'cannot unilaterally affect any state of affairs.'" Finally, process thinkers conclude that "all positive and negative experiences are conserved and reconciled in God's own conscious life" and that "God 'include[s] in himself a synthesis of the total universe'" (110). The certainty of ultimate universal salvation is now replaced by a positive *hope* for such a triumph.

Not surprisingly, process concepts have come under attack from both classical theists and nontheists alike. Theists have objected to what they term as a caricature of the process concept of divine power. They suggest that the process exponents could as easily have justified the distinction between coercive and persuasive power by using terms such as "productive power," "sustaining power," or "enabling power," rather than prejudicial terms such as "totalitarian" and "monopolistic" (111). Classical theists defend their own view that God's all-powerful nature does not exclude others from also having power. They also criticize process thinkers for debasing divine goodness by giving it an aesthetic rather than moral orientation. If the principal purpose of undergoing suffering is to attain a richer and more variegated life experience, and if it is God who either caused or allowed such suffering in the first place, then God's ultimate morality is brought into question. Can mere aesthetic aims justify so much suffering? They can and do, reply the process theists, for aesthetic values are a more inclusive category than moral values. But as Peterson et al. highlight, "hanging on the issue of whether God is morally good is the related question of whether he is worthy of worship" (111).

These three global theodicies offer divergent views of the dilemma of evil in relationship to God and humans. Another vision with unique characteristics is presented in the Vedas, the ancient texts of India, and may be called the monotheistic *Vedic theodicy*. The great saint Chitraketu summed up the tenets of this theodicy at the time of receiving what was apparently a most unjust judgment for a minor indiscretion. Though destined to return back to the kingdom of God, he was condemned instead to take birth as a great demon opposed to God's servants. His response is recorded in the *Bhagavata Purana* (6.17.21-24):

> The Supreme Personality of Godhead is one. Unaffected by the conditions of the material world, He creates all the conditioned souls by His own personal potency. Because of being contaminated by the material energy, the living entity is put into ignorance and thus into different conditions of bondage. Sometimes, by knowledge, the living entity is given liberation. In *sattva-guna* [goodness] and *raja-guna* [passion], he is subjected to happiness and distress.
>
> The Supreme Personality of Godhead is equally disposed toward all living entities. Therefore no one is very dear to Him, and no one is a great enemy for Him; no one is His friend, and no one is His relative. Being unattached to the material world, He has no affection for so-called happiness or hatred for so called distress. The two terms happiness and distress are relative. Since the Lord is always happy, for Him there is no question of distress.

Although the Supreme Lord is unattached to our happiness and distress according to karma, and although no one is His enemy or favorite, He creates pious and impious activities through the agency of His material potency. Thus for the continuation of the materialistic way of life He creates happiness and distress, good fortune and bad, bondage and liberation, birth and death.

O mother, you are now unnecessarily angry, but since all my happiness and distress are destined by my past activities, I do not plead to be excused or relieved from your curse. Although what I have said is not wrong, please let whatever you think is wrong be pardoned.

Before we can correctly evaluate Chitraketu's humility and surrender to supreme destiny, it behooves us to firmly grasp the philosophy behind his response. The *Bhagavad-gita* (5:15) may elucidate the matter more fully: "Nor does the Supreme Lord assume anyone's sinful or pious activities. Embodied beings, however, are bewildered because of the ignorance which covers their real knowledge." In his commentary to this verse, A. C. Bhaktivedanta Swami Prabhupada fully unpacks the essential aspects of the Vedic theodicy:

The Sanskrit word *vibhu* means the Supreme Lord who is full of unlimited knowledge, riches, strength, fame, beauty and renunciation. He is always satisfied in Himself, undisturbed by sinful or pious activities. He does not create a particular situation for any living entity, but the living entity, bewildered by ignorance, desires to be put into certain conditions of life, and thereby his chain of action and reaction begins.

Here, the Supreme Lord is portrayed as an all-powerful, omniscient being, who dwells undisturbed beyond the created universe. Each creature's particular condition is not determined by God, but by the creature itself. The living entity *freely* selects its own situation; the wrong choice or desire which will lead to eventual suffering is due to his own *ignorance*.

One may ask how this ignorance arises. Prabhupada explains,

"A living entity is, by superior nature, full of knowledge. Nevertheless, he is prone to be influenced by ignorance due to his limited power. The Lord is omnipotent, but the living entity is not. The Lord is *vibhu*, or omniscient, but the living entity is *anu* or atomic. Because he is a living soul, he has the capacity to desire by his free will." The soul, the true essence of each entity, shares God's superior nature. But unlike the infinite Godhead, the individual soul is atomic. Hence, though the soul is constitutionally full of knowledge, it is prone to being covered by ignorance due to its limited power.

How does the transcendental soul become embodied? By misuse of its free will. But how, one may ask, can a pure soul which shares the same nature as God become so confused? Though godly by nature, the soul is not omnipotent. Bewilderment causes the soul to become embodied and identify with the circumstantial material body and the temporary misery and happiness of material existence. Again, could not the omnipotent God arrange to influence the soul to choose right instead of wrong and thus avoid suffering altogether? Prabhupada answers this critical question:

> The Lord is the constant companion of the living entity as Paramatma, or the Supersoul, and therefore He can understand the desires of the individual soul, as one can smell the flavor of a flower by being near it. Desire is a subtle form of conditioning for the living entity. The Lord fulfills his desires as he deserves: Man proposes and God disposes. The individual is not, therefore, omnipotent in fulfilling his desires. The Lord, however, can fulfill all desires, and the Lord, being neutral to everyone, does not interfere with the desires of the minute independent living entities. However, when one desires Krsna, the Lord takes special care and encourages one to desire in such a way that one can attain to Him and be eternally happy.

Significant free will requires a substantial degree of independence. God does not interfere with the living entity's choices. But critics may judge God harshly for failing to give sufficient wisdom to the soul. How can an all-good and compassionate God remain aloof while the creatures he created undergo such severe suffering? This crucial question is covered by the Vedic theodicy with its conception of God as the indwelling witness or Supersoul that accompanies the individual soul throughout its journey in material existence. Much as the Holy Spirit of Christianity pervades and sustains the faithful, the Paramatma (Supersoul) is the Vedic expansion of the Godhead who responds internally to the individual's needs. God in his kingdom may thus continue his sublime existence while his expanded representation personally looks after the created beings so long they are within this universe. Through scriptural guidance, saintly association, and divine inspiration from within, the individual is gradually led back to the path of goodness, to be freed eventually from the law of karma and the cycle of rebirth. Once purified of all mundane desires, the soul is free to return back home, back to Godhead.

Prabhupada summarizes:

> Therefore the embodied soul, by his immemorial desire to avoid Krsna consciousness, causes his own bewilderment. Consequently, although he is constitutionally eternal, blissful and cognizant, due to the littleness of his existence he forgets his constitutional position of service to the Lord and is thus entrapped by nescience. And, under the spell of ignorance, the living entity claims that the Lord is responsible for his conditional existence.

We return now to our story of the saintly Chitraketu, hopefully with a better understanding of the philosophy that underlies his response to an unjust curse. A pure devotee of the Lord like King Chitraketu is never afraid or sorry. Rather, he addressed the female judge as "mother," a sign of utmost respect, and accepted the curse, thinking himself faulty. He never uttered a word in retaliation. Parvati (the lady judge who actually condemned Chitraketu) was the consort of the exalted Lord Shiva. Upon observing Chitraketu's exemplary behavior, Lord Shiva remarked that the condemned king had actually excelled the glory of the auspicious Parvati's beauty and power. She and her excellences were all defeated by Chitraketu's pure devotion. Lord Shiva exclaimed:

> Devotees solely engaged in the devotional service of the Supreme Personality of Godhead, Narayana, never fear any condition of life. For them the heavenly planets, liberation and the hellish planets are all the same, for such devotees are interested only in the service of the Lord. (*Bhagavata Purana* 6.17.28)

Parvati might naturally have inquired how devotees become so exalted. This verse explains that it is due to their total dependence upon and surrender to God. They do not mind reverses in life, no matter how severe or unfair. Rather, such reverses are seen as a boon, for they propel the devotee towards the Lord. Queen Kunti, the mother of Arjuna (who heard the *Bhagavad-gita* spoken by Krishna directly), remarked to Lord Krishna, "I wish that all those calamities would happen again and again so that we could see You again and again, for seeing You means that we will no longer see repeated births and deaths."

Vedic theodicy thus takes a greater-good approach to why God should allow suffering in this world. Elevated personalities like Chitraketu and Kunti can recognize the value of such suffering as inducements for total surrender. Others may have to learn by the 'school of hard knocks.' But, if the cause of suffering is misuse of one's own free will, and if, due to ignorance, one is unable to recognize one's mistake, what possibility is there of becoming knowledgeable? It may be suggested that undergoing punishments is itself a learning experience. It makes one search for the causes, and it is often humbling. Humility and inquiry can prepare one for finding ultimate solutions. And what of those who suffer what appears to be pointless evil? The Vedic response is that nothing happens by chance: one's actions in this life or in past lives are all noted and judged according to the laws of karma. The task of accounting for every minute action of each and every living creature may boggle our finite brains, but for the unlimited and all-knowing Godhead, everything is possible. The death of an apparently innocent infant or the devastation of an entire town's population may thus be explained.

The Vedic theodicy, along with other theodicies and defenses, presents a powerful case that evil is necessary to achieve a greater good. Whatever may be one's theistic persuasion, inquiry into the nature of evil is neither a useless endeavor nor one to be feared. As theists throughout the centuries have demonstrated, there is ample reason in believing that God has substantial moral grounds for allowing evil to exist. Rather than lessening our belief in God, such inquiries can strengthen our faith.

CHAPTER 4

Religious Language:

How Can We Speak Meaningfully of God?

Shabda, eternal, divine truth in sonic form, is the authoritative basis of Sanskrit, India's primeval religious language. Though originally meant to convey spiritual truth, the use of Sanskrit gradually devolved from the purely spiritual to include the temporal. On the other hand, our 'younger languages,' without distinctively 'religious' grammar or vocabulary, have had from the start to make use of very *ordinary* words to explain *extraordinary* realities (e.g., God, heaven). Terms like 'Heavenly Father' and 'heaven' are derived from the finite world, yet are meant to describe a transcendental reality. Just how do words about God actually derive their meaning? Theologians and philosophers alike have had to wrestle with understanding the meaning of the language used to express religious beliefs as part of the comprehensive understanding of the beliefs themselves.

Thinkers throughout history have accepted the veracity of religious language, but recently—early in this century—a group of philosophers known as *logical positivists* have strongly contested its validity. Under the influence of the scientific method, they have demanded that religious language must be tied to empirical observation, much as scientific language is. Peterson et al. sum up their "verifiability principle": "A statement is a genuine factual assertion if, and only if, there could be empirically observable states of affairs that would show it to be either true or false" (141). Because most religious subjects deal with matters beyond empirical observation, theological language was judged by logical positivists to be unverifiable and thus "pure nonsense." The further implication is that all attempts to defend theism (and, they would concede, *attacks* on theism as well) are also ruled out since nonsensical language cannot be debated.

Antony Flew tightened the positivists' view of cognitive meaning in his formulation of a "falsifiability principle." Simply stated, Flew contended that the religiously faithful will continue to modify and qualify their claims and proclamations, rather than allow them to be falsified by empirical evidence. By never holding steadily to any definite state of affairs which might disprove their theological contentions, religious believers "kill their own claims by a thousand qualifications" (142).

Such positivist critiques helped to fuel significant debate in which the parties divided over whether theological language was meaningless or meaningful. R. M. Hare sided with those who considered religious language cognitively meaningless. He based his view on the perception that religious discourses expose a "blik," his term for believers' predisposed world views by which they resolutely deflect empirical observations. Bliks are ways of interpreting facts, and the believer uses such bliks to fortify his belief that God exists. Hare's theory seems rather naïve, for faced with substantiated contradictory evidence, even 'true believers' would likely change their minds.

Basil Mitchell championed the opposing view that religious utterances are cognitively meaningful and can, in fact, meet the positivists' criteria (143). To establish his view, Mitchell uses an interesting parable about a member of a resistance movement meeting a stranger who impressed him deeply. The stranger tells the partisan that he too is a member of the resistance and, in fact, is the leader of it. The partisan is never to doubt this even though the facts may appear otherwise. The partisan is deeply impressed by the stranger, even when, as it turns out, the stranger's activities appear paradoxical. Sometimes the stranger is seen aiding the resistance and other times apparently acting in collusion with the occupying power, yet under all circumstances the partisan's faith remains unshakable, leading his friends to wonder what it would take for him to withdraw his confidence.

As Mitchell observes, though the partisan's trust is firmly established, he is not unaffected by the stranger's ambiguous behavior. Rather, this "trial of his faith" ultimately makes his trust more resolute. It is not, as certain positivists would assert, a *blind* faith. Rather, as with many other factually significant, nontheological claims, theological propositions are not conclusively falsifiable. Scientific claims may need to be altered as ever-new evidence is admitted; so might theological views change, Mitchell would say, were there significant-enough reasons. If the articles of a religious believer's faith are unalterable, it is because there is no sufficient contradictory evidence. But while acknowledging the sense of Mitchell's strategy, it would seem that he has not explained clearly enough the relationship between the degree of faith and the evaluation of facts.

John Hick attempted to extend the principle of verification to "the exclusion of rational doubt" (144). To do this, he suggests a parable whose ending depends upon what will finally be discovered in an afterlife. The expectation of such observational afterlife experiences logically justifies the cognitive significance of theological statements. But the weakness of Hick's "eschatological verification" theory is that it presupposes an afterlife which we presently cannot verify.

Ironically, the verification/falsification issue has been abandoned by most thinkers because its own foundational proposition can itself not be evidentially verified. Furthermore, though they hold science and scientific language as a paragon, many scientific statements have been and continue to be accepted as truth without the necessary empirical evidence to substantiate them. This is equally so for numerous other assertions used in our daily life. Even though it has been more or less abandoned, the positivist dialect has at least forced theologians to consider the *factual* content of their transcendent reality claims. But "God-talk" can never be considered exclusively fact-talk, nor can the assessment of the *truth* of religious language be equated with the evaluation of its *meaning.*

Many philosophers felt that the positivist debate failed to deal with the essential aspects of religious language. Following the lead of Ludwig Wittgenstein, they saw language as a social phenomenon adaptable to the ever-changing purposes of human beings. This "functional analysis" tried to ascertain the function of religious language.

For R. B. Braithwaite, a pioneer in the field, religious claims are essentially *moral* rather than factual statements. Whether or not such statements are true is not as important as whether they express moral intentions and reinforce moral behavior. Donald Hudson points out the obvious weakness of this position, calling it a violation of the "depth grammar" of religion (146). In a sense, Braithwaite's mistake parallels the positivists': both circumscribe the meaningfulness of God-talk by their prejudiced views.

Another functional analyst, Paul van Buren, suggested that human language can be categorized into a variety of "language-games": the language of science, the language of romance, and the language of religion (146). Each language-game has its own set of 'rules,' unspoken understandings between the linguistic-game players. For example, the 'passion' of a romantic couple is something quite distinct from the 'passion' of Christ. Van Buren locates religious language "at the edges of [the] language" map. At the center of the map are the languages of science, history, and common sense. We generally stay in this central 'safety-zone.' At the distant edges are those language usages which stretch our sense of reality: puns, poetry, paradox, *and* God-talk. Each of these derives extraordinary value from ordinary terms.

Thus, Christian "edge-talk" may include such utterances as "God raised Jesus from the dead," a statement which performs an entirely different function for believers than for historians. Every religion is replete with many such examples.[1] As pleasing as edge-talk seems to be, it runs into some serious opposition. Unlike the linguistic groups which lend themselves more easily to empirical analysis, religious language holds itself aloof from the questions appropriate to these others. "Religion cannot ask whether its most fundamental term—the term *God*, which constitutes and governs its whole field of discourse—can play by the rules of other fields in which naming and referring are key techniques" (147). By neglecting its informative dimension, the functional analysis of religion nearly surrenders to the very charge leveled by positivists—that it is cognitively meaningless. In this regard, if religious discourse were to establish its own set of clear standards it would at least allow a certain degree of objective analysis. Otherwise, by placing God-talk at the edge of the linguistic fringe, van Buren practically acknowledges the positivists' assumption that science and its linguistic counterpart occupy stage-center.

Van Buren also seems to ignore the multi-dimensional function of religious language; in addition to making metaphysical assertions, it is used to relate historical events and describe daily ritual. Besides, traditionalists who hark back to the beliefs of Thomas Aquinas would say that van Buren's assessment fails to acknowledge the common perception of most believers, namely, that religious language conveys specific factual truths.

Great medieval thinkers like Thomas Aquinas never doubted that religious language was meaningful, but realized the difficulty of accounting for its meaning. Peterson et al. summarize Aquinas's now classic theory of "analogy" or "analogical predication":

---

[1] An instance from the *Ishopanishad*: "The Supreme Lord walks and does not walk. He is far away, but He is very near as well. He is within everything, and yet He is outside of everything."

A predicate term in a sentence attaches some property, relation, or activity to the subject term. Thus, predicates define or characterize the subject in particular ways. "God is just" [is a typical example] . . . Aquinas held that when a word—say, the word *just*—is applied both to a created being and to God, it is not being used *univocally* (i.e., with the exact same meaning) in the two instances. Yet, neither is the word being used *equivocally* (i.e., with two completely different meanings), as when "hot" is used to apply to pepper corns and race cars. . . . Because of this similarity, the predicate term *just* is not used equivocally, but because of the differences between God and finite human beings, it is not used univocally either. As Aquinas indicates, the word is used *analogically*. It is the similarity within difference and difference within similarity that allows the analogical use of the same term in two different contexts. (138)

James Ross has appreciated Aquinas's traditional analogy theory in terms of modern-day semantics. On one hand, the theory of analogy avoids anthropomorphism, the idea that God and other creatures differ only in degree, which would allow both to be spoken of univocally. On the other hand, it also avoids agnosticism, the view that God is so different that we cannot know anything intelligible about him, which would demand that we use equivocal language when describing him. The analogy theory treads the middle path, allowing God to be described in human language without necessarily equating him with ordinary creatures. Ross explains that analogies are often invoked in everyday speech, as for example, "Susan's anger is volcanic" (139). Here, the comparison is between two familiar easily observable items. The difficulty arises when the analogy is between such familiar realities and the transcendent reality of God. A viable religious language theory must account for this connection. To do so, Aquinas formulated rules for analogy, with the rule called the *analogy of proper proportionality* considered to be the basis of his theory.

Underlying this rule is the basic understanding that God and humans share similar attributes and activities. For example, both

God and Socrates are *wise*; therefore, the predicate term *wise* is not used equivocally. Yet God, unlike Socrates, has infinite wisdom; hence, the predicate term *wise* cannot be used univocally. Hence, Aquinas's theory holds: God and creatures have qualities in common *in proportion to* their respective modes of existence. Though Aquinas's theory has endured through the centuries, it has not gone unchallenged. Frederick Ferré and other critics maintain that the theory does not provide any substantial knowledge of God (140). Ferré sets up an equation between God's wisdom proportionate to his infinite nature, equaling Socrates's wisdom proportionate to his finite nature. The defect, Ferré complains, is that there are not just one, but two unknowns—God's wisdom and his infinite nature.

Ross minimizes Ferré's 'mathematical' critique as inappropriate; Aquinas intended to explain religious language's meaningfulness by pointing out the similarity to ordinary language, not by stipulating some exact mathematical relationship. Ross also blames Ferré for demanding that Aquinas's theory provide information about God. Aquinas's purpose, he explains, is not to spell out the exact nature of God, but merely to explain how predicates applied to God have meaning. These analogies can assist us in understanding what statements about God mean while avoiding the pitfall of ascribing mundane attributes to God.

The deep conviction shared by Aquinas and his Scholastic contemporaries has held sway more or less until the present day. Verificational analysts have doubted the cognitive meaning of religious discourse, and functional analysts have identified uses which are basically noncognitive. But as we have seen, these contemporary philosophers have not provided fully convincing arguments. Thus, despite these wholesale challenges, the meaningfulness of religious language has been upheld by most modern philosophers. Many, however, object to the *literal* interpretation invoked by Aquinas's theory, which they find to be too anthropomorphically suggestive. Instead, they prefer a *symbolic* interpretation of religious discourse, while still seeking to establish the bonafide cognitive value of God-talk.

Symbolists insist that God is fundamentally symbolic and that all predicates that describe God are irreducibly metaphorical. God's infinite transcendent status, they believe, is violated by all literal discussion. Men like Paul Tillich go so far as to assert that God is not *a* being at all, but is rather "the Ground of Being" (149). And Tillich is not alone; the anti-literal viewpoint virtually dominates twentieth-century thought. Though they may ally themselves with Aquinas on the principle of religious language's validity, they differ totally in their ultimate conclusion. If God is so far beyond any literal description, Aquinas would undoubtedly wonder, *what*, if anything, do symbolic statements reveal about God?

Present traditionalists are willing to concede that religious language can be symbolic as well as literal. Aquinas never suggested that God was in any way a limited being, as Tillich accuses. But both in their own ways agree that God is special— Aquinas by the analogy of proper proportionality, and Tillich by demanding symbolic usage only.

Yet Tillich is clearly pantheistic, while Aquinas is not. For Tillich there is no question of the existence of a God who can accommodate the predicated qualities, but to Aquinas, the religious assertions of believers have meaning if, and only if, the God they describe exists. For Tillich, God is so unlike any other creature, and literary language so incapable of proper description, that symbolic language alone is possibly useful. But if literal statements are ruled out, and if symbolic statements are at best approximations, then how can the normal tests of the fidelity of language—"logical relations to one another, such as contradiction, negation, and implication"—be applied? As Peterson et al. explain, "to say symbolically 'God is love' is not to contradict 'God is hate' or 'God is cruel,' because relations such as contradiction just do not apply" (151). Symbols are by definition vague and relative in value. Tillich may be satisfied that symbolism says something about how God can be encountered, but Aquinas would demand that all statements be spelled out in literal terms and subjected to reasonable tests of truth and falsity.

In a view that echoes Aquinas's sentiments, William Alston suggests that God can indeed be described, but that our concepts about God require refinement. Alston admits to the limitations of language. A "subject-predicate" pattern does not lend itself well to explaining a God that is Being-itself. We humans love, but God *is* love. Essence and existence are one in God, creating problems for language which makes a distinction between the object and the properties which predicate it (150). Though the "mode of signification" (the form of our language) may be defective, it may still be used to signify the "perfection" (the reality about which we speak), providing we purify the terms we use of all their mundane connotations.

Certainly, Alston's approach will be more appealing to traditionalists. Unlike Tillich, he affirms that language can meaningfully describe the divine being. Yet one wonders how much purification terms and concepts must undergo before he would deem them sufficiently purged of mundane creature-like attitudes. If this cleansing process goes too far, one could easily move into the pantheistic ground espoused by the pan-symbolists. The ideal which Alston imagines, and one which Aquinas would find quite pleasing, is the refined means of communication found in India's ancient Vedas and employed even to this day by Vedic practitioners.

Vedic practitioners accept *shabda* as external transcendental sound, coming directly from God, and expressed in the form of Vedic mantras (invocations that situate the mind in spiritual consciousness). If this proposition can be established, many of the criticisms against man-made God-talk will be avoided. It must be emphasized that the outset that establishing Vedic authority is not intended to diminish the relevance of other religious traditions; rather, many of the arguments given hereafter may equally support their position.

A proper understanding of Vedic linguistics must begin with its origin—God. In the theistic Vedic conception, God is envisioned as a Supreme Personality, whose perfect and complete attributes are reflected proportionately in humans and other creatures ("God created humankind in his image"). We are reminded here of Aquinas's analogy of proper proportionality. Vedic texts give the exact mathematical equation for comparing God with created beings: they may have up to 78% of the attributes of God (50 of his 64 principle qualities), but in minute quantity. Shared attributes include compassion, gentleness, magnanimity, power, etc., all in minuscule proportion. Qualities which are specific to God include full cognizance, and the ability to create innumerable universes and award salvation. Symbolists like Tillich would argue that such a description of God violates his transcendence. The Vedic response is to explain God in three aspects, one of which—Brahman—is more akin to Tillich's Ground of Being: "Learned transcendentalists who know the Absolute Truth call this nondual substance Brahman, Paramatma or Bhagavan" (*Bhag. Pur.* 1.2.11). This all-embracing Vedic version of the three-in-one concept requires a lengthy discussion beyond our present scope; suffice it to say that the Bhagavan feature, the Supreme Person, possesses *spiritual* names, *spiritual* form, *spiritual* qualities, and is capable of *spiritual* activities, none of which fall under the limiting influence of time or space.

But our primary interest here is religious discourse or transcendental sound—*shabda*. The positivists' demand for verificational proof has already been set aside by most modern thinkers, so we shall not spend further attention refuting what would be their unreasonable demand that all the above be proven by empirical observation. Rather, let us proceed to illuminate the topic at hand. We may recall van Buren's theory of language-games and religious edge-talk. Peterson et al. have asked whether religion was prepared to "play by the rules of other fields in which naming and referring are key techniques" (147). One might ask at this point, by which rules must religion play? Will scientists play by any other rules than their own? And if not, who has made the arbitrary judgment that their rules are superior to any others? Sanskrit, the language of the Vedas, has set for itself such an exhaustive system of rules that to master its grammar alone, it is said, takes twelve years. Analysis of the cognitive value of Vedic discourse is certainly possible, but one should do it according to the 'rules of the game.' One must prepare himself by spiritual discipline, and take great pains to ensure the purity of one's consciousness while proceeding with one's studies.

The most pure sound is the sound of God's name. Hebrew forefathers deemed it so sacred, they forbade even its utterance. The Vedas inform us that God's name is identical with God himself, much as the apostle John affirms, "In the beginning was the Word, and the Word was with God, and the Word was God." We learn from the *Padma Purana*:

> The holy name of Krishna is transcendentally blissful. It bestows all spiritual benedictions, for it is Krishna Himself, the reservoir of all pleasure. Krishna's name is complete, and it is the form of all transcendental mellows. It is not a material name under any condition, and it is not less powerful than Krishna Himself. Since Krishna's name is not contaminated by the material qualities, there is no question of its being involved with maya [illusion]. Krishna's name is always liberated and spiritual; it is never conditioned by the laws of material nature. This is because the name of Krishna and Krishna Himself are identical. (qtd. in *Chaitanya-charitamrita*, Madhya-lila 17.133)

The phenomenon described above is quite distinct from what we normally encounter. Under normal circumstances, an object is not the same as the words which represent it. But the Puranic text informs us of an entirely different state of affairs where an object and its sound representation are nondifferent. The sound representation of the Lord is nondifferent from the Lord because all the Lord's potencies are invested in his holy names; the Lord and his representation in sound are absolute knowledge.

"All very well and good," one may say, "but what happens when such pure sound enters the material realm? And, are only God's names invested with such transcendental potencies? What of religious discourse in general?" To answer these questions we must first understand how transcendental sound descends from the spiritual realm. In the *Bhagavata Purana* (3.26.32-3), the fundamental principles of material nature are discussed in the context of creation. The purport by A.C. Bhaktivedanta Swami Prabhupada describes the transmission of *shabda*:

> When egoism in ignorance is agitated by the sex energy of the Supreme Personality of Godhead, the subtle element sound is manifested, and from sound come the ethereal sky and the sense of hearing.
>
> Persons who are learned and who have true knowledge define sound as that which conveys the idea of an object, indicates the presence of a speaker screened from our view and constitutes the subtle form of ether.

> [Purport] It is very clear herein that as soon as we speak of hearing, there must be a speaker; without a speaker there is no question of hearing. Therefore the Vedic knowledge, which is known as *sruti*, or that which is received by hearing, is also called *apaurusa*. *Apaurusa* means "not spoken by any person materially created." It is stated in the beginning of *Srimad Bhagavatam*, *tene brahma hrda*. The sound of Brahman, or *Veda*, was first impregnated into the heart of Brahma, the original learned man (*adi-kavaye*). How did he become learned? Whenever there is learning, there must be a speaker and the process of hearing. But Brahma was the first created being. Who spoke to him? Since no one was there, who was the spiritual master to give knowledge? He was the only living creature; therefore the Vedic knowledge was imparted within his heart by the Supreme Personality of Godhead, who is seated within everyone as Paramatma. Vedic knowledge is understood to be spoken by the Supreme Lord, and therefore it is free from the defects of material understanding. Material understanding is defective. If we hear something from a conditioned soul, it is full of

defects. All material and mundane information is tainted by illusion, error, cheating and imperfection of the senses. Because Vedic knowledge was imparted by the Supreme Lord, who is transcendental to material creation, it is perfect. If we receive that Vedic knowledge from Brahma in disciplic succession, then we receive perfect knowledge.

The above texts and purport provide important clues to answering our questions. We learn (a) that not only God's name, but also the Vedas, his speech, are transcendental; and (b) that the Vedas were entrusted to Brahma, the first created being.

It is not entirely clear yet from these hints whether or not the originally pure Vedic sounds become contaminated once they are received by Brahma, nor is it clear what will be their fate once he communicates them. To clear these doubts we must understand how Brahma manifested the Vedic sounds he received from God. But before we proceed further, a word of caution: The Vaishnava theistic followers of the Vedas do not understand the communication between God and Brahma as a symbolic description. The Supreme Being is a Supreme Person, and Brahma, his first created being and his representative, is also a real person. Vedic assertion does make use of symbolism and other forms of speech. But even these are understood within a very traditional theistic concept, far away from the Ground of Being Tillich mentions. Bearing this in mind, we may read (from *Bhag. Pur. 3.12.47*):

Brahma's soul was manifested as the touch alphabets, his body as the vowels, his senses as the sibilant alphabets, his strength as the intermediate alphabets and his sensual activities as the seven notes of music.

[Purport] In Sanskrit there are thirteen vowels and thirty-five consonants. The vowels are *a, a, i, i, u, u, r, r, l, e, ai, o, au*, and the consonants are *ka, kha, ga, gha*, etc. Amongst the consonants, the first twenty-five letters are called the *sparsas*. There are also four *antahsthas*. Of the *usmas* there are three *s*'s, called *talavya, murdhanya* and *dantya.* The musical notes are *sa, r, ga, ma, pa, dha* and *ni.* All these sound vibrations are originally called *shabda-brahma,* or spiritual sound. It is said, therefore, that Brahma was created in the Maha-kalpa as the incarnation of spiritual sound. The *Vedas* should be vibrated as they are, although they are symbolically represented with letters which are known to us materially. In the ultimate issue there is nothing material because everything has its origin in the spiritual world. The material manifestation is therefore called illusion in the proper sense of the term. For those who are realized souls there is nothing but spirit.

Here we have the answer to our questions about what happens to pure sound when it enters the material realm. It does not become contaminated, because Brahma, its original recipient, is himself the "incarnation of spiritual sound." Brahma prepared himself for enlightenment, and to ensure that the messages he received were transmitted with equal fidelity, he instructed his students in the purifying techniques he had undertaken. Brahma is the first of the learned teachers, and the line of disciplic succession originating from him is known as the *Brahma-sampradaya.* The Vedic system is to capture the essential truth of the Vedas in mantras that can be transmitted exactly by teachers to their students. The Vedic mantras are themselves transcendentally potent, inspired as they are by the vibration of supernatural (*aprakrita*) sound, which descends in the chain of disciplic succession from the Lord to Brahma, from Brahma to Narada, from Narada to Vyasa, and so on. Without being inspired or initiated by a bonafide representative in the line of succession, one cannot possibly properly understand the import of Vedic teachings. Because these mantras spring from the spiritual platform, they surpass all lower stages of consciousness, namely sensual, mental, and intellectual. That is not to say that they cannot be evaluated, but merely to indicate that the full appreciation of their value can only be realized by a trained devotee.

Our conclusion is that religious language, be it Vedic or otherwise, is certainly meaningful. God *can* be described, but we must refine our concepts about him. This is best done by taking advantage of sources like the Vedic literature, such as *Brahma-samhita* and the *Bhagavata Purana*. These texts, which can be referenced by people of all religious persuasions, provide evidence from beyond the plane of the mundane world.

The descent of *shabda* from the spiritual realm is a manifestation of God's mercy upon the living entities entrapped by material conditioning. *Anavrittih shabdat*, "liberation by sound," is a reversal of the process of material entanglement. According to the Vedas, as explained above, the material manifestation began with sound; hence, one can be liberated from it through sound as well. But one's perception of that sound must be purified by spiritual understanding. Purified perception of transcendental sound will free our consciousness of all inebriates, and in such a heightened state we will be able to experience the Personality of Godhead face to face.

CHAPTER 5

Miracles:

Does God Intervene in Earthly Affairs?

- 5-year-old Melinda sits spellbound watching *Sesame Street* muppets Miss Piggy and Big Bird use human intellect and discourse to resolve a recent problem in their relationship.

- Philosopher Spencer Wiseman sits nervously at the edge of his seat watching *Star Trek* Captain Kirk reintegrate a dissolved Starship Enterprise.

- Christians world-wide observe Easter, remembering Christ's miraculous resurrection.

What have these three in common? Philosopher Wiseman would easily discern that in each instance nature's laws have been violated—animals don't talk, totally disintegrated objects do not reintegrate, and the dead do not come back to life three days later. Wiseman was quite pleased with his daughter Melinda's fascination with the talking animals. She wasn't bothered by the fact that animals don't reason or talk. Besides, her absorption with the TV allowed him the peace of mind to focus on completing the final chapter of his book, "Miracles and the Problem of Evil." In addition, he himself occasionally gave reason a rest in order to enjoy the *Star Trek* serial. He had no difficulty willingly suspending his disbelief long enough to enjoy the space odyssey.

But somehow the vision of millions worldwide believing the

impossible fantasy of the resurrection disturbed him. There was nothing wrong, he reasoned, with *Sesame Street* or *Star Trek*—just a bit of healthy fun. But that thinking adults, some scientists included, could actually affirm such a *supernatural* event as a genuine piece of *history*, troubled him greatly. In the face of wide-scale gratuitous evil, how could they persist in maintaining such a deception?

Miracles are a problem not only for our fictitious philosopher Wiseman, but for many modern thinkers as well. Nonbelievers and even many religiously faithful seriously wonder if God can actually intervene in earthly affairs. Miraculous occurrences form a central element of the founding of all the major theistic religions whose members claim that God continues to have a hand in directing human history through miraculous means in order to accomplish his divine purposes. The rise of modern science, however, accompanied with critical thought and comparative religious dialectics, has raised serious doubts concerning the authenticity of miracles. If such arguments cannot be reasonably refuted, they will continue to win more and more converts to their side, seriously diminishing the ranks of theistic believers. By comparing and contrasting the basic arguments for and against the actual historical occurrence of miracles as "unexplained events," we will be in a position to better evaluate the believers' and unbelievers' positions on the relationship between the question of miracles and the problem of evil. Finally, we shall apply the same arguments to an evaluation of the recent "milk-drinking" miracle reported by millions of Hindus world-wide.

The question of whether or not miracles are possible can be approached by posing a subset of three related but distinct questions:

> Under what conditions can a person reasonably maintain that certain unusual events have actually occurred as reported? Under what conditions can a person reasonably maintain that an event could have

no natural explanation? And, under what conditions can a person reasonably maintain that God was directly involved in bringing about a given occurrence? (159)

Dealing with the first question, Are there sufficient conditions under which a Christian could justifiably believe that Jesus *actually* came back to life after he had been dead for three days, or that Jesus *actually* turned water into wine as reported? Antony Flew is the most influential philosopher to argue that there are not (159). He advocates that belief should be proportionate to the evidence provided. Dead men stay dead and water remains water—it has always been that way and will most likely continue to be so. If "violations" of these natural occurrences have only *personal* testimony from the distant past as their single evidence, such evidence will always be significantly weaker than the *natural laws* which it contradicts. Such testimony cannot hold up to the scientific test of *repeatability*: we have no way of re-staging the circumstances as they were said to have occurred in the past to observe whether divine intervention occurs again. Regarding the Jesus miracles, Flew therefore concludes that "'no matter how impressive the testimony might appear, the most favorable verdict history could ever return must be the agnostic, an appropriately Scottish 'not proven'" (160).

As can be imagined, Flew's naturalistic critique has had a chilly reception amongst theists. They fault Flew for ruling out nonnatural factors such as the inerrancy of biblical statements guaranteed by its divine origins. Furthermore, these believers argue, past miracles are prototypes to identify God's ongoing intercession in human events. Why should Flew dismiss such nonnatural evidence altogether?

Peterson et al. point out that such criticism is misguided. Flew is only considering the issue on the basis of historical (natural) evidence alone, and is not making any statement about others' beliefs in nonnatural criteria. In fact, Flew is offering such believers a means to strengthen their claims: if they can establish the said miracle on "natural" grounds, they will at least have proven to nonbelievers that the event did actually occur. Still, Flew's line of reasoning is not beyond reproach. Imagine a large group of internationally renowned physicians reporting that they have all observed a severely deformed and withered leg instantaneously return to normal size and shape (161). According to Flew's understanding, unless this phenomenon can be demonstrated to repeatedly reoccur, we cannot accept it as fact. Of course, it must be considered that natural laws do give us a sense of what we can and cannot expect to happen. Though this may have no bearing on examples like the withered leg, there is some merit to bearing this proposition in mind when studying supposed miracles.

The basis for Flew's contention is evidence; specifically, *reported observations*, which are dependent on belief-forming faculties (162). But observational reports are subject to the shortcomings of such faculties. This must be borne in mind when we study any evidence. Furthermore, natural laws are constantly changing in keeping with new information. To reject a reported miraculous occurrence because it violates current natural laws does not allow for the possibility that these laws may change in the future. Flew's contention, therefore, is certainly not airtight.

Richard Swinburne reminds us that relevant *physical traces* provide an especially important body of evidence. X-rays, photographs, and video tapes of a reported occurrence go a long way towards removing doubts. Given the availability of reliable evidence (trustworthy belief-forming faculties as well as physical traces), we may judge that the natural laws have indeed been reversed. But to what extent do one's prior beliefs affect the judgment? It is hard to imagine that they would not; hence, in the absence of "hard" evidence, it would not be unfair to suspend final judgment with respect to the accuracy of any report. And conversely, if we have personally observed a counterinstance (one that challenges our current natural laws), or if others with sound observational faculties have observed such a counterinstance, or if we have very reliable physical traces relating to a seeming counterinstance—given any one or combination of these possibilities, we have justifiable grounds to believe that the event has indeed occurred as reported. Critics might still insist that there has never been a compelling basis for accepting the occurrence of nonrepeatable events. But this again misses Flew's real point. "Flew is not simply claiming that there has never in fact been a compelling basis for accepting the occurrence of a nonrepeatable counterinstance. His claim is that there could *in fact* never be such a basis" (163-4). This leaves the door open to the possibility of establishing a counterinstance in the future. In conclusion, every reported miracle must be judged on a case-by-case basis, taking into account the above criteria as a means of judgment. Though Flew and his supporters argue otherwise, they have not conclusively demonstrated that miracles are impossible.

The above analysis provides a means to judge the reliability of reported counterinstances. Bearing what we have learned in mind, we may now turn our attention to assess whether such counterinstances may actually defy all natural explanation. This collapses into whether we can judge an event to be directly an act of God. Some would immediately object that the primary purpose of natural science is not to assess actual causes. "[R]ather, [it] is to map regularity patterns between certain types of occurrences and certain sets of causal conditions, and then use these patterns to formulate general explanatory (and thus predictive) laws" (164-5). Furthermore, as Peterson et al. have already pointed out, since science is always digging up new information and revising its natural law definitions, it is impossible to ever state absolutely that there can be no natural explanation in the future for a miraculous event.

Some philosophers disagree. Though they grant that laws may constantly be revised, there may be certain occurrences which can never be given a natural explanation. Swinburne argues in favor of this proposal (165). He reasons that there are certain laws that are so well entrenched that to change them will upset the whole status quo of the scientific worldview. Bringing the dead back to life or transforming water to wine cannot be accommodated by any change of the "laws of nature." Hence, Swinburne argues, such occurrences could justifiably be considered unexplainable events.

Margaret Boden further substantiates Swinburne's conclusion by using the example of a leper whose missing fingers reappear instantly in the presence of doctors or TV cameras. To adjust natural formulas sufficiently to accommodate such an anomaly would be to render the predictive powers of such laws useless. Peterson et al. again invoke the warning that science is always advancing into the realm of ever-new discoveries, which keeps open the future possibility of natural explanations for presently unexplainable events. Then, as if to answer themselves, Peterson et al. state what would probably be the position of Swinburne and Boden: science must either "modify its laws to accommodate the occurrence, or . . . affirm the adequacy of the laws and declare the event permanently unexplainable" (166). In some conceivable cases, the latter would be preferable.

Some would prefer not to concede this point. They would suggest, instead, a type of delay tactic. The apparent miracle might simply be a "freak event." Before investigating further, wait for other similar events to occur. But this, as R. F. Hollande points out, not only casts doubt on the event, but on the existing natural law against which it is being judged. Not so, insist those who demand *repeatability* as a necessary criterion of judgment. Why, they argue, should a person have to choose either one of the two options presented by Swinburne and Boden? Instead, why not select both the "law" and the counterinstance, and continue to affirm the adequacy of the existing law while searching for new or modified laws to accommodate the unusual occurrence?

Though it is possible to make a case for miracles as

unexplainable events, religious believers want a more explicit declaration of God as the causal agent. What would please them most is to be able to establish sufficient grounds to undermine even the strictest naturalist.

Tan Tai Wei strives for this goal by suggesting that repeated requests by Jesus, and by others later, for God's intervention, have met with regular miraculous responses (167). If no natural cause of matching regularity can be found, it would be the more rational posture to acknowledge supernatural intervention. Grace Jantzen argues likewise. Persons like Jantzen and Tan are strong in their insistence that under the above conditions, everyone should admit God's causal relationship with the event.

Yet there is a powerful argument that looms against this understanding. Evidence supporting a claim cannot be considered in isolation; all other related data must also be considered. If we assume God's existence, and therefore that it is God who is responding to the fervent appeals for intercession in the case of a terminally ill patient, why then does God not intercede by eliminating widespread evil? To claim God as the causative agent for miraculous healing is also to attach God to all other relevant data (i.e., evil). It is unlikely that Jantzen or Tan would be satisfied with such a conclusion. But their proposal is a knife that cuts on both edges. If it can be assumed that God's existence is not compatible with all that is experienced (i.e., evil), then it can also be concluded that it is not God who healed the individual. Under these circumstances, how can either Jantzen or Tan demand that the only rational conclusion for certain occurrences is that God acted directly?

Many believers are not so insistent as Jantzen and Tan. For others, it is enough that they themselves can justifiably claim certain events are direct acts of God. Such a believer might assume a defensive posture, arguing that unless evidence to the contrary is provided, they have a right to their claim. Other believers offer a more positive solution, what might be termed the "divine-pattern" thesis (169). God's acts in this world follow a certain pattern, and, if it can be discerned that a particular occurrence fits within this pattern, the event can be attributed to God. Of course, this thesis does not rule out the possibility that God can act outside of previously demonstrated patterns. In such a case one would admit that there is insufficient reason at present for thinking that God is involved, without totally ruling out the possibility. Alternatively, if, for example, a healing came in response to a petition, the believing petitioner would only assert that the healing fit an accepted divine-action pattern, giving sufficient reason to believe God to be the cause, but at the same time not insisting that God was forced to fit into a specific pattern and thus respond to the petition. Of course, all of this assumes that believers accurately interpret the action patterns attributed to God and described by their scriptures. Not infrequently, they misread their tradition and make unsupported claims.

Returning to the question of godly intervention and the problem of evil, Why does God seem to intervene in some instances but not in others? As we have already explained in a previous chapter, God cares for everyone, yet is self-limiting to provide an opportunity for moral improvement. It is not beyond God's ability to remove all ills from the world, but that would not ensure the ultimate benefit of humankind, nor would it be compatible with God's gift of free will. Still, it does seem that God is acting whimsically by helping some and not others. More particularly, as process theist David Griffin asks, Why doesn't an all-powerful God act more frequently "'in order to prevent particularly horrendous evils'" (171)?

Believers have many possible responses. For instance, situations that may seem analogous to us may not be so from God's viewpoint. Similarly, God is under no obligation to resolve problems in ways which *we think* are appropriate. Despite such responses, evil remains the Achilles' heel for most theists, leaving many to wonder if God does in fact intervene. To the same degree that a believer excuses God from acting against evil, such a believer has less reason to expect godly intervention in any particular situation. And if a believer claims that God's actions are inscrutable, the same limitation applies to predicting the nature of God's intervention.

Regarding God's inscrutable actions, millions of Hindus recently proclaimed September 21st, 1995 "World-wide Miracle Day." Worshipable deities in temples ranging as far afield as New Delhi, Hong Kong, Sydney, Los Angeles, Chicago, London, and Nairobi were said to be accepting milk spoon-fed to them by their devotees. The apparently supernatural phenomenon began in India when a devotee dreamed that a local deity wanted milk. When the unidentified man held a spoonful of milk near to the deity, the milk suddenly disappeared. Word spread quickly, and when it was picked up by the media and reported to the Indian public, droves of devotees headed for their local temples to personally experience the miracle. Indian newspapers reported the phenomenon:

- "'Milk-drinking' deities unleash mass hysteria" *(The Pioneer)*
- "Gods feast on the milk of human faith" *(Business Standard)*
- "Reaching God the milky way" *(National Herald)*
- "A miracle for believers and a mystery for atheists!" *(Free Press)*
- "A reawakening for Hindus, claims VHP" *(The Telegraph)*
- "Scientists dismiss it as mass hysteria" *(The Statesman)*
- "Holy smoke: Psychiatrists believe this is only hysteria" *(The Asian Age)*
- "Awestruck devotees see second coming of avatar" *(The Telegraph)*
- "Milk miracle catches fancy of United Kingdom Catholics" *(The Telegraph)*
- "The gods prefer milk, but they're saying no to Coke" *(The Asian Age)*

The above headlines indicate the mixed reception accorded the reported miracle. The phenomenon was so widespread and received so much media attention, it forced every Hindu to confront his or her faith and decide whether or not the miracle was actually possible. Scientists, scholars, politicians, and laymen—all were polled for their opinions. The final truth may be difficult to assess, considering the large amount of data which would need to be evaluated. Considering the parameters of this present study, we can at best subject some of the general findings to the various arguments suggested above.

We may recall Flew's edict that belief should be proportionate to the evidence provided. Our "milk-drinking" miracle has ample *personal testimonials*—millions in fact! The occurrence passed the test of *repeatability* again and again. Unlike a past event whose circumstances cannot be re-staged, the recent occurrence repeatedly took place under similar circumstances. In each case a natural law appears to have been violated. Inanimate objects do not normally "drink." Yet that is exactly what millions say took place on September 21st, as the following testimonials confirm:

> Hong Kong Hindu temple head priest: "I was praying at about 4:00 p.m. yesterday when I had a hint that maybe we should try feeding Lord Krishna. Five minutes after a little girl started feeding the statue with milk using a spoon, the idol started drinking."

> Montgomery County, Maryland Hindu temple devotee Mrs. Aruna Sharma: "I didn't believe it until I came here. Now I believe it." *(Beyers)*

> Haashad Parikh, trustee at the same temple: "I have a Ph.D. in mechanical engineering, and I can't explain it. I went back to my office and said, 'I'm not insane, but this is really happening.'" *(Beyers)*

As can be expected, there was no dearth of disbelievers, as the *Washington Post* reported:

> A reporter held a teaspoon of milk up to the statue's trunk and observed the fluid being absorbed into the statue, which temple officials say is made of marble. There were no visible holes in the statue.

But the stone could be porous, because when the reporter carelessly spilled milk on Ganesh's potbelly, it quickly disappeared as well.

Shawn Carlson, a physics professor at the University of San Diego who investigates reported miracles: "I've heard of statues crying, but never ones drinking milk."

Richard Muller, physics professor at the University of California, Berkeley: "This may be a natural phenomenon that no one paid much attention to before because no one tried to feed the statue milk. But I suspect they'll know soon enough, when the milk begins to sour."

But to the fifty-five thousand who visited the Birla Temple in New Delhi, and to the Indian Government itself, which ordered an emergency shipment of 100,000 quarts of milk, these comments seemed of little value. After all, for those who are devotees, there are ample scriptural references that describe similar miracles. Deities have been known not only to eat and drink, but to walk and talk. A. C. Bhaktivedanta Swami Prabhupada, in his commentary to the medieval Bengali classic *Sri Chaitanya-charitamrita* (*Madhya-lila* 5.97), explains this phenomenon in connection with a marble deity of Lord Krishna speaking to his devotee brahmana:

> The conversation between Lord Sri Krishna and the brahmana is proof that the Lord in His *arca-murti*, or form made of material elements, is not material, for those elements, although separated from the Lord, are also part of the Lord's energy, as stated in Bhagavad-gita. Because the elements are the Lord's own energy and because there is no difference between the energy and the energetic, the Lord can appear through any element. Just as the sun can act through the sunshine and thus distribute its heat and light, so Krishna, by His inconceivable power, can appear in His original spiritual form in any material element, including stone, wood, paint, gold, silver and jewels, because the material elements are all His energy. The *sastras* (scriptures) warn, *arcye visnau sila-dhih*: One should never think of the *arca-murti*, the Deity within the temple, as stone, wood, or any other material element. Because of his advanced devotional position, the younger brahmana knew that although the Deity of Krishna appeared

to be stone, He was not stone.

As such, the Deity can act exactly as the Lord did in His original form as Krishna. Lord Krishna was talking to the young brahmana just to test his knowledge about the *arca-vigraha*. In other words, those who have understood the science of Krishna—Krishna's name, form, quality and so forth—can also talk with the Deity. To an ordinary person, however, the Deity will appear to be made of stone, wood or some other material. In a higher sense, since all material elements ultimately emanate from the supreme spiritual entity, nothing is really material. Being omnipotent, omnipresent and omniscient, Krishna can deal with His devotees in any form without difficulty. By the mercy of the Lord, the devotee knows perfectly well about the Lord's dealings. Indeed, he can talk face to face with the Lord.

With such scriptural backing, it is no wonder that Hindus were confident that their experience was indeed a supernatural event. And yet, if we may recall, Flew's intention is not to contest belief systems, but rather to demand that they be supported by evidence. Such support will only strengthen the believer's position. *Reported observations*, however, are subject to the shortcomings of *belief-forming faculties*. As we shall see, the shortcomings of such faculties may play an important part in our analysis of this event. After all, the elderly Chinese Buddhist in Bangkok may not have 20/20 vision. But how could millions have been deceived? What of the photographic records and video tapes devotees the world around took to preserve the memory of those cherished moments? These are the type of "relevant physical traces" Swinburne considers an especially important body of evidence. But were these gathered in a truly scientific manner? Shawn Carlson, the physics professor cited above, opines that the statues could be made of stone that contains tiny capillaries capable of drawing liquid from the surface. In fact, the Indian Government decided that its Department of Science and Technology should investigate the matter, and their findings seem to confirm Carlson's hypothesis. An Associated Press release reads:

Their scientists offered milk mixed with colored pigments to an idol in a New Delhi temple. Although it disappeared from the spoon, it soon coated the idol. The scientists credited the "miracle" to surface tension, saying molecules of milk were pulled from the spoon by the texture of the statues.

The federal minister for welfare, Sitaram Kesari accused two right-wing groups of starting the rumors to capitalize on Hindu nationalism and win next year's general elections.

To accept the scientists' evaluation would mean that all the belief-forming faculties of the millions of Hindus were untrustworthy. And the A. P.'s final statement even suggests foul play. Certainly we cannot rule out either possibility. There is also the fact that one's prior beliefs can affect one's judgment; this would be equally true of the scientists and the believers. Yet there are Hindus whose experiences parallel those of the Department of Science and Technology. Take, for example, this report of a temple president from South India, himself a qualified engineer:

One of our members called up and said that their metal Ganesh deity was drinking milk. I asked him if he could bring his Ganesh deity to the temple. Accordingly, he brought the deity. He showed how, when the milk in the spoon touched the tip of the trunk of the deity, the milk gradually rose and flowed towards the point of contact and soon the spoon was almost empty. Yes, what they said was happening to the milk in the spoon! It was rising up and flowing over and soon the spoon was almost empty. Anyone would get amazed when he saw the milk and the spoon empty. Then I asked the member to leave the Ganesh deity for the night with us.

After he left, all the temple devotees tried one by one and were amazed to see the phenomenon. After many spoons were fed it was noticed that the tray holding the Ganesh deity was slowly getting filled with milk. So he was not actually drinking! The milk was just flowing over the rest of the deity and collecting below. While flowing over the body, the layer is so thin that even milk doesn't show its whiteness. Only wetness shows.

One of the devotees scooped up a spoonful of milk in the tray and started offering. That was also accepted. Then the devotees offered the spoon to the rat Vahana that was at the feet of the deity (Ganesh is said to ride about on a rat). He also drank the same way. Thus doubt began. Then we touched the spoon to the side of the stainless steel vessel and the milk drained out of the spoon in the same way. Then there was a paperweight made of glass on the table. As soon as we touched the spoon full of milk at a point on the bottom half of the paper weight, we were surprised to see the milk emptying even faster than with Ganesh.

We tried on a picture of Ganesh. Yes, it happened there also. Then we tried on the reverse side of the same paper, and it happened. Sometimes it would not flow on the first attempt. Then we found out why. First, somehow the contact point that you are touching should become wet. Once it is wet, the milk starts flowing. So this adds to the mystery for an ordinary person who thinks that some personal prayer on the part of the devotee is involved (i.e., in the beginning, the deity refused to drink, but once prayed to, he started drinking). They wetted him first by tilting their spoons slightly over him as they could not bear that their Ganesh deity is not accepting when everyone else's is. After that, hundreds of people continued the exercise.

Then we recalled what we had studied in our school about capillary action due to surface tension of liquids, wherein the liquid can rise against gravity under certain conditions. A capillary action was taking place. A very thin layer between the spoon and the object you are touching is formed and capillary action begins to drain the milk from the spoon, molecule by molecule, in a chain.

In some temples there was a great stampede and people were even on the altar. In the course of this rush, most of the milk that was flowing down spoon by spoon, was being taken out little by little by the touch of the devotees' hands and on their feet. So it appeared that the deity had consumed the liquid. Of course in the case of marble or stone deities, some absorption also takes place.

The above statements clearly indicate that there is indeed a natural explanation for the milk-drinking event. This explanation has sufficiently satisfied the scientifically minded, that they feel no need to seek out some new scientific explanation, and certainly no need to postpone their conclusion until certain further facts surface.

But the scientific community is not entirely aligned on one side. There are those who suggest that a specific occurrence can be seen as a physical or a spiritual event depending on the level of realization of the observer. Consequently, the deities may actually be drinking milk while some physical process may also be taking place (e.g., absorbing capillaries in the marble, etc.) This higher-realm theory is not new. In fact, the entire basis of Vedic cosmography is founded on this principle. The arguments are long and well thought-out. Our present analysis, unfortunately, does not allow us to do more than acknowledge the substantial body of ancient texts that support this contention, providing a basis for modern, scientific explanations.

Viewed in such a light, the milk-drinking phenomenon might be seen to fit within the "divine-pattern" thesis. Yet on closer examination one wonders if it does. There are scriptural injunctions regulating the methods of temple worship. Reports of the deities drinking often indicate that no rules or regulations were observed. Of course, it is entirely possible that God in his deity form may transcend his own rules. But then he would be violating the action patterns attributed to him and described by scriptures. Furthermore, what are the moral implications if God drank from the hands of the pious *and* the sinful? Many faithful Hindus, observing this fact, have been unwilling to accept this event as a supernatural occurrence, and these same persons also wonder what ultimate good has come of it. They acknowledge that individual believers' faith has certainly increased, and many who were not believers have now become converts. But has the overall suffering of humankind been reduced? Has evil diminished in any noticeable way? Those Hindus and non-Hindus who disbelieve this miraculous claim, find the lack of tangible evidence of increasing good since the time of the supposed miracle to be a telling fact.

The last word on the milk-drinking miracle has by no means been spoken. There will undoubtedly be arguments made from both sides for years to come. Skeptics and believers alike have justifiable grounds for substantiating their positions. Perhaps it is best, in conclusion, to adopt a thoughtfully balanced view like that of Michael Byrd, a Ph.D. candidate of religion and ethics at Vanderbilt University:

> The line between confessions of religious belief and scientific explanations is not at all clear to me at this point. The hypothesis that milk is "absorbed" into some stone rather than "drunk" by gods seems as open to question as the explanations that Hindus seek to offer (i.e., the gods wanted to bestow blessings on those who comply). The main difference seems to turn on one's views of nature: qualities that "innate" or "unintentional" matter possesses vs. extra-material or higher intentionalities. Other than that, I find the speculation about "capillary channels" most persuasive only if I choose to accept the idea that nothing else in the world could possibly be happening.

CHAPTER 6

Life After Death:

Are There Reasons for Hope?

Near the city of Xian, the ancient northern capital of China, an army of terra-cotta soldiers and horses have been unearthed, signs of an ancient king's burial site. In Egypt, thousands-of-years-old mummies, taken from the pyramids, were found amidst elaborate provisions for the departed persons' comfortable afterlife. These testimonies bear witness that life after death was a serious concern for the peoples of these ancient civilizations. And so it is, even today. A modern Taiwanese burns paper money and offers bowls of food for the benefit of his departed ancestors, a Christian lays his loved one to rest in a grave to await resurrection, and the Hindu cremates the deceased family member's body so that the soul may not be obstructed from its next reincarnation. Even the atheist, by a speech, plaque, statue or otherwise, seeks to preserve something—the accomplishment, teachings, values—of the individual who has departed.

All these speak of a common phenomenon: an unwillingness to allow life to end with the body's demise. Exactly how one treats the dead will reflect one's philosophy about life and, of course, the possible afterlife. Can an individual actually survive death? And if so, are there any "proofs" of life after death, either philosophical or experiential?

The consideration of life after death entails two

presuppositions: (a) the existence of an extremely powerful God who facilitates survival after death, and (b) a type of being that can live subsequent to its death. Arguments in previous chapters have established the reasonable assumption that such a powerful God exists. But we have not yet investigated and identified the nature of a being that would enable it to exist after its death. We will, therefore, turn our attention first to this topic before assessing the question of life after death.

One possible approach is to differentiate our true personal identity from our physical being. Simply put, it is incorrect to say, "I body"; we say, "My body." Neither can a person be identified with the mind, for memories, thoughts, and other products of the mind may be altered or lost without loss of personal identity. Our mental states may be useful in ascribing personal identity, but do not in and of themselves constitute personal identity.

Another possibility is that we are "a nonreducible, ultimate, unanalyzable self" (179). The language we commonly use reveals this truth: we do not say that we "have" a self, but that we "are" a self. The method of knowing our self is through intuitive self-awareness or through having experiences. The self is the subject of such experiences and the "agent of thinking, remembering, feeling, and understanding." This notion has strong backing. First, each of us has our own individualized set of beliefs, desires, intentions, and feelings. Access to this set is private information that others can come to know of only indirectly, unlike the physical body which is publicly perceptible. "Since the public and the private are contradictories," Peterson et al. conclude, ". . . introspective reports about ourselves and our mental states cannot be about something public."

A second evidence that the self is our basic identity is connected with individual freedom and its consequence, moral responsibility. For humans to be truly free, there must be something within us which is not part of any physical, deterministic causal chain. This 'something' must be that which is responsible in making moral choices, since to do so is a prime feature of our person.

A third argument advanced on behalf of the notion that we are the self is that the body can simultaneously house multiple persons, or, rather, personalities. This argument has been advanced by a number of philosophers and is of great concern to psychiatrists in general. Whether they view that there are actually different persons occupying the same body, or that it is actually one person with a number of personalities, is to some extent irrelevant to our purpose. In either case, it seems clear that the body cannot be considered the locus for personal identity, since a normal, psychically healthy person intuits himself as ultimately being one person, rather than the schizophrenic state of being many.

Finally, there is a fourth argument which alleges the existence of human paranormal powers (181). Telepathy, clairvoyance, and psychokinesis entail communication without the need of intermediate physical agencies, and are therefore concepts quite incompatible with a materialistic conception of the mind as the self.

The above four kinds of evidence lend support to the view that there is some sort of nonphysical self quite distinct from, though dwelling within, the body. This self, or soul, experiences self-awareness, memory, conceiving, and emoting. While these functions are enacted through the gross and psychic bodies of the individual, it may be that they originate in the soul proper, meaning that these functions might occur independent of the body. The consequences of this conclusion for life after death are obvious. Death is a termination of the physical state which would not affect the nonphysical entity. The soul, along with whatever else is nonphysical, would survive death. This allows for a quality of afterlife which may, in many ways, resemble our present state, since there could still be self-awareness, memory, conceiving, and emoting, along with all that these imply.

The soul concept is not without its critics. Suggestions that psychic functions operate independently of the brain run counter to much of modern psychological and physiological research. There is evidence that the physical process of heredity plays an important part in determining mental ability and function. Furthermore, it is a commonly observed fact that damage to the brain affects these subtle, psychic functions. Finally, researchers hypothesize that certain mental abilities, like memory, are locatable in the brain and that other functions, like intelligence, are at least associated with specific cerebral hemispheres.

These strong arguments plunge soul/self supporters into a serious dilemma: they must either ignore altogether modern scientific findings, or recant their own claim. Neither alternative appears desirable, making reconciliatory explanations a necessity. One possible solution is to acknowledge the brain's involvement with psychic functioning in this life, while affirming that at least some of these functions may continue to be accomplished by some sort of ethereal body that accompanies the soul in the afterlife. Otherwise, to deny the possibility of these functions in the afterlife would mean severely limiting the quality of such afterlife by depriving the soul of any meaningful function.

This leads to the next obvious question: What exactly is the nature of such an afterlife? Peterson et al. point to two possible schemata (182). In the first, the soul unites with a body, either spiritual or material (the latter being the case for those who believe in reincarnation). Each of these possibilities is difficult to verify. A spiritual body would exist on another, spiritual plane; a reincarnated body would, it is suggested, not allow for remembrance of previous life's experiences, making it more of a *new* birth rather than *re*birth. A second schema presents the concept of the soul disembodied either temporarily until united with a body, or permanently. Scenarios are presented by advocates of both schemata in support of their beliefs.

All the above contentions rest on a common principle, namely, that personal identity is equated with the soul, a nonmaterial entity. Their problematic nature has led certain modern philosophers to seek personal identity in our psychophysical unity. One contemporary view is called the Identity Theory or Central State Materialism. According to this theory, humans are merely physical organisms. Mental states are nothing more than brain processes. "The mind is what the brain does"; states of consciousness are thus irreducibly psychical (183).

This view has come under attack for violating "a traditional principle (called Leibniz's principle of the identity of indiscernibles), two things are identical only if every property of one is also a property of the other" (183-4). The problem with the Identity Theory is that two things having different properties are nevertheless considered identical: mental states are nonspatial and private, while the brain is spatial and public. Identity Theorists defend by stating that one cannot expect total identity between two things when applying the properties of one would be meaningless applied to the other (i.e., mental states being spatially limited). But then, if Leibniz's principle is not adhered to, exactly what criteria will be used to judge identity?

Modern-day reductionists like Douglas Hofstadter go as far as to suggest that a living entity's existence can be ultimately reduced to nothing more than neural firings:

> Taken individually, these neural firings are random and meaningless, but statistical regularity reveals patterns that encode the information necessary for the organism to respond interactively to other patterns of symbols in its environment. When the patterns of firings are interpreted at the highest levels, we give them meaning, and these meaning-assigned patterns become alternative ways of explaining who we are. (184)

Hofstadter uses the analogy of an ant colony to represent a high-level structure that ultimately consists of nothing more than the random motions of individual, unintelligent ants. He concludes that we are nothing more than programmable machines, replicable in the future by computers. Thus, Hofstadter's model has no real role for a 'person' other than the convenience the term affords in giving explanations.

The reductionist's view, though thought provoking, is rather unsettling. Peterson et al. point out that the relation between computer and brain seems to be simulation, not replication. But more important, by replacing the humanistic concept of person with artificial intelligence, this view "leaves us mechanistic shipwrecks, reacting to events in ways that can be described as having meaning, but really do not" (185).

Surprisingly enough, the radical reductionist view does not discount the possibility of life after death. If we assume the existence of an all-powerful, omniscient God (though such an assumption seems rather at odds with such a materialistic view), it is possible to imagine being recreated, since God's task would be nothing more than reproducing the 'programs' we once were, and fitting these programs into suitable hardware. It is doubtful that such a concept would satisfy those seeking solace in the idea of an afterlife. But taking this science fiction-like idea to its conclusion, would the recreated person be the same as the deceased? One might argue that the recreated is neither spatially nor temporally continuous with the deceased (186). Reductionists would respond that this is not a necessary criterion. In support of their defense, Peterson et al. remind us that magicians have the ability to at least make us believe that they have recreated things which previously disappeared. A further example is the spatiotemporal continuity we accord characters in television serials, their disappearance and reappearance being interspersed by commercials or week-long segmentation. As these examples would suggest, the deceased and the recreated are identical if the internal states of consciousness and personality traits or patterns are the same. In any case, what emerges from all of this is that whether we take personal identity as soul-based, or see it according to the mechanistic view of the reductionists—both allow for the possibility of life after death. If we grant that life after death is indeed possible, is there any reason to think that it actually occurs? This will be our next subject of inquiry.

We shall examine our subject by two methods: *a priori* philosophical arguments and *a posteriori* arguments derived from various experiences. The first *a posteriori* argument involves near-death or life-after-life experiences, in which the person either nearly dies or dies and is resuscitated. Though ample testimonies of both sorts exist, they have been challenged on the grounds that they are nothing more than hallucinations caused by physiological disorders. But these reports are often astonishingly accurate (something one would not expect from a drugged person) (188). In fact, the reports often include accurate information of events taking place in nearby places other than in the room in which the person's body is situated. Again, it might be argued that these descriptions represent some type of religious vision, perhaps induced by the person's prior beliefs. Yet they do not resemble normal religious experiences. As Raymond Moody attests in his study, the descriptions he gathered made no mention of such traditional themes as heaven or hell. Again, there are also reports of seeing relatives, a fact which in and of itself would not be surprising, except that such relatives were often previously unknown.

The after-death body has been variously described as "invisible," "able to move through physical objects," and "weightless (floating)," while still retaining the powers of perception (188). All of this indicates a sound basis for concluding that death has been survived, particularly because these experiences are marked by two essential elements: recognition of personal identity and recollection of the past.

A second *a posteriori* argument has evolved from psychical reports concerning mediumistic communication with deceased persons. Much of this research has been discounted, however, because of the many clear cases of fraud. There are also clinical objections. The medium may be projecting his or her own thoughts, or those of others seeking the help of the medium on behalf of the deceased person. Yet certain instances (as for example when a deceased person reveals a fact which he or she alone could have known) seem to lend weight to this argument. Still, even here there is room for doubt. Revelations of this sort are often cryptic and vague; the medium's extensive explanations often become more weighty than the few obscure words of the deceased. Besides, with little detail of the communicant's present circumstance, it is difficult to surmise if their present status represents a truly meaningful existence.

A third and final *a posteriori* argument arises from the claim that certain persons have actually come back to life. Jesus is a prime example, along with the Apostle Paul's theological explanation of the resurrection. Such claims have a two-fold dependence: that we accept (a) certain theological assumptions, such as God's existence, and (b) the accuracy of the reported event.

The question which remains after examining these *a posteriori* arguments is not whether such reported experiences are factual, but exactly how they should be interpreted. By contrast, *a priori* arguments are by definition based upon reasoning and hence are more easily analyzed. We shall examine three of them.

The first was articulated by Thomas Aquinas (190). He asserts that God made us for an ultimate end, namely happiness. Since God's creation cannot be in vain, and as it is clear that we do not enjoy perfect happiness in this life, it necessarily follows that we must continue to live after death. This thesis can be questioned by referring to Aristotle, who held that happiness is not a momentary feeling of pleasure, but the state one experiences in leading a virtuous life. The implication is that one can achieve happiness in this life. Aristotle emphasizes the use of reason and contemplation, but Aquinas finds our present knowledge of God by reason imperfect. Since perfect happiness is achieved through perfect knowledge or contemplation of God, we must live beyond death to experience this perfect state.

Aquinas's argument rests on the conception that we shall have lived in vain if we cannot achieve our ultimate end. Peterson et al. try to redefine the ultimate end in more relative terms (190). Why, they ask, would a person's life be in vain if they had *limited* knowledge, happiness, and realization of God? Is Aquinas's insistence on perfection an arbitrary assumption? And, would God not fulfill our endeavors on his behalf, though it now represents but a modicum of success? And if God would do so, where would that fulfillment take place—in this lifetime, or in the next? This argument leads to many such questions.

Immanuel Kant advanced a second *a priori* proof, using an argumentative method similar to the one put forward by Aquinas. Kant reasons that moral perfection is a final goal, but one which humans cannot achieve in this life; hence, there must be an afterlife (191). Moral law tells us that we must strive to achieve the highest good. But since this highest good is humanly unattainable, how can we be commanded to strive for it? The same relativist response offered to Aquinas can again be used: Why must one be able to achieve the *highest* good in order to be commanded to act morally? Kant would respond by explaining that the moral law demands that we *attain* the highest good, not merely *strive* for it.

The third *a priori* argument was formulated by Plato who postulated that the soul is immortal because it is imperishable, it is imperishable because it is indestructible, and it is indestructible because it is simple (191). But why, Peterson et al. question, does the soul's *simplicity* imply indestructibility? Simple things can be destroyed. Still, it is admitted that Plato's argument would probably hold true if the soul is left alone, for without an outside destroying agent, there would be nothing to cause its destruction.

The *a priori* and *a posteriori* arguments for immortality will seem more convincing to those who have already adopted a theistic world-view. The soul's immortality and its life after death are generally important elements of most theologies. This is especially true of the Vedic world-view. Let us briefly review the concepts already examined in this chapter, but this time using the Vedas as our point of reference. Before doing so, however, we wish to differentiate the monotheistic Vedic conception from the monistic, Vedantic brand of Hinduism, whose goal is much akin to Mahayana Buddhism. The monistic Vedantic version prescribes that the individual self merge with the Supreme Whole. Hence, this version has little importance in our present discussion, for the self-as-an-individual ceases to exist, much "like putting a drop of water into the ocean" (177). The goal, for these monistic Vedantists, is that the self should *not* survive death. "Indeed, desire to preserve our identity is the root of our problems."

Monotheistic Vedantists, on the other hand, strongly affirm personal life after death. That the self, or soul, is separable from the body is a fundamental concept explained at the beginning of the *Bhagavad-gita* (2:13, 16, 22):

> As the embodied soul continually passes, in this body, from boyhood to youth to old age, the soul similarly passes into another body at death. A sober person is not bewildered by such a change.
>
> Those who are seers of the truth have concluded that of the nonexistent [the material body] there is no endurance and of the eternal [the soul] there is no change. This they concluded by studying the nature of both.
>
> As a person puts on new garments, giving up old ones, the soul similarly accepts new material bodies, giving up the old and useless ones.

These verses establish that the soul separates from the body not only at death but within a single lifetime. Though we change bodies continuously, from childhood to youth to old age, we still remain the same person, capable of remembering the changes. There is a distinction between the knower and the known, the seer and the seen, the soul or self and the body it inhabits. Contemplation of this distinction leads to realization of one's actual identity. A. C. Bhaktivedanta Swami Prabhupada explains:

One can perceive one's self identification and feel positively that he exists. He may not feel it very abruptly, but by using a little intelligence, he can feel that he is not the body. He can feel that the hand, the leg, the head, the hairs and the limbs are his bodily parts and parcels, but as such the hand, the leg, the head, etc., cannot be identified with his self. Therefore just by using intelligence he can distinguish and separate his self from other things that he sees. So the natural conclusion is that the living being, either man or beast, is the seer, and he sees besides himself all other things. So there is a difference between the seer and the seen. (Purport, *Bhagavata Purana* 2.2.35)

The mind along with the intelligence and false ego comprise the subtle body of the living entity. At death, when the gross body is shed, the subtle body carries the soul to its next gross body. Thus, according to the Vedic conception, the process of thinking, including such acts as remembrance, is not dependent upon the brain made of gross matter, but is a function of the mind, which exists as subtle matter independently of the brain. This idea is also acknowledged as a legitimate response to modern scientific research, which indicates that mental and intellectual abilities are locatable in the brain and can be affected by brain damage. Damage done to the brain may temporarily disrupt the functions of the ethereal body but does not destroy it.

The future destination of the soul after death is determined by its consciousness just before departing the body. This is explained in the *Bhagavad-gita* (8:6):

Whatever state of being one remembers when he quits his body, O son of Kunti [Arjuna], that state he will attain without fail.

[Purport] The process of changing one's nature at the critical moment of death is here explained. A person who at the end of his life quits his body thinking of Krsna attains the transcendental nature of the Supreme Lord, but it is not true that a person who thinks of something other than Krsna attains the same transcendental state. This is a point we should note very carefully. How can one die in the proper state of mind? Maharaja Bharata, although a great personality, thought of a deer at the end of his life, and so in his next life he was transferred into the body of a deer. Although as a deer he remembered his past activities, he had to accept that animal body. Of course, one's thoughts during the course of one's life accumulate to influence one's thoughts at the moment of death, so this life creates one's next life. If in one's present life one lives in the mode of goodness and always thinks of Krsna, it is possible for one to remember Krsna at the end of one's life. That will help one be transferred to the transcendental nature of Krsna. If one is transcendentally absorbed in Krsna's service, then his next body will be transcendental (spiritual), not material. Therefore the chanting of Hare Krsna, Hare Krsna, Krsna Krsna, Hare Hare/ Hare Rama, Hare Rama, Rama Rama, Hare Hare is the best process for successfully changing one's state of being at the end of one's life.

This commentary suggests two possible future scenarios for the departed soul, both falling within Peterson et al.'s first schema (182). In one, the liberated soul enters the kingdom of God where its spiritual body is manifest. In the second, the conditioned soul must reincarnate in another material body according to its past karma. Peterson et al. suggest that each possibility is problematic. In the former case they assume that the spiritual body will exist on a different spatiotemporal plane. Vedic texts, however, say otherwise, as in this description by the sage Narada of his own liberation (*Bhagavata Purana* 1.6.27-28):

> In due course of time I, who was fully absorbed in thinking of Krsna and who therefore had no attachments, being freed from all material taints, met with death, as lightning and illumination occur simultaneously.
>
> Having being awarded a transcendental body befitting an associate of the Personality of Godhead, I quit the body made of five material elements, and thus all acquired fruitive results of work [karma] stopped.

Narada's statement sheds light on a number of interesting points. First, there is recognition of personal identity and recollection of the past, both clear indications that it is the same individual who was present before death and who survived afterwards. Unlike his previous body, Narada is awarded a transcendental body invested with three primary transcendental qualities: eternity, freedom from material modes, and freedom from reactions of fruitive activities. Narada also explains in later texts that he travels "everywhere without restriction both in the transcendental world and in the three divisions of the material world." Certainly this defies Peterson et al.'s understanding of a "different spatiotemporal plane."

Under normal circumstances death plunges the soul into forgetfulness. Still, it is the same individual self enwrapped in the subtle body of mind, intelligence, and false ego who is reborn, not born new. Though specific remembrance of the past life's circumstances may be denied the reborn, the unfinished desires and karmic reactions are 'remembered,' for it is these which propel one to act in the next birth. In the earlier commentary to *Bhagavad-gita* (8:6), Prabhupada mentions Maharaja Bharata, who took rebirth as a deer but was able to remember his past. Again, though it is certainly an unusual occurrence, this differs with Peterson et al.'s conception of reincarnation.

There is yet another possibility for the departed soul, one that Peterson et al. hint at in their other schema: "the soul continues to exist disembodied" (183). According to the Vedic literature, when the soul fails to acquire either a material or spiritual body due to various causes, it may remain for a time as a disembodied spirit, commonly known as a ghost. Ghosts lack the gross physical body required to fulfill desires; hence their constant attempt is to inhabit the bodies of others and through such possession fulfill their own desires.

A most interesting near-death experience is reported in the *Bhagavata Purana's* Sixth Canto. While lying on his deathbed at the end of an especially sinful life, the dying Ajamila watches as the order carriers of the death god Yama begin to drag his soul with its subtle body from the core of his heart. Ajamila has used his final breath to call his son whom he had providentially named Narayana, a name of the Supreme. The Lord's holy name attracts the Lord's order carriers who then forbid Yama's servants from carrying the soul away for punishment. A debate ensues during which God's messengers explain that a person who chants God's holy names at the time of death is exonerated from all karmic reactions. Ajamila's life is spared and he returns to normal consciousness to tell his story and mend his ways. Whether or not one accepts that this narrative factually occurred, one might argue that Ajamila's vision is colored by his previous religious beliefs. This type of argument would appeal to a nonbeliever.

Another *a posteriori* example, also from the Sixth Canto, is the sage Narada's use of mystic power to summon the departed soul of the son of a grieving king and his queen. The child returns to life and speaks words of deep philosophical import in order to console his parents before he again departs. Yet another instance occurs in the Tenth Canto when Krishna travels to the kingdom of Yama to bring back the dead son of his teacher. Of course, such *a posteriori* "claims" presume, as Peterson et al. would point out, certain theological understandings as well as faith.

Regarding the *a priori* arguments for life after death, the Vedic authorities would find Aquinas's arguments quite acceptable. They would disagree with Kant's estimation of human inability to achieve moral perfection. In fact, the Vedas teach that moral perfection is a prerequisite for eternal life, not the consequence of it. Vedic authorities would fully endorse Plato's argument that the soul is immortal because it is imperishable, because it is indestructible, and because it is ultimately simple. This is reminiscent of the description of the soul found in the *Bhagavad-gita*, Chapter Two.

The Vedic conception, like other theistic world-views, sees immortality as an essential element of the eternal relationship between the individual and God. Except in the case of the anthropological materialist who denies the existence of God altogether, spiritualists and materialists alike have reasonable grounds to think that life after death is possible. For the spiritualist, the soul is the true person that survives death; for those who believe solely in the materialistic constitution of the individual yet still allow for the existence of God, God is capable of recreating a person exactly as the person existed before death. Either view contends that life continues to exist. This was the view in ancient China, Egypt, India, Greece and elsewhere, and it remains so for most of humanity today.

CHAPTER 7

Religion and Science:

Compatible or Incompatible?

The river Ganges, flowing from the heartland of the Himalayas across the plains of northern India, provides numerous places of pilgrimage for India's religious population. Indeed, one can become 'purified' by a mere dip in her waters. Of equal sanctity are the cows that roam freely, grazing by her banks. They are considered pure in all respects; even their dung and urine are valued for their prophylactic quality. Householders living on the Gangetic plains since ancient times have worshiped the Ganges and the cows, but when the British became rulers they viewed such Hindu traditions with skepticism. Much to their surprise, however, they found that only Ganges water remained potable during the six-week ocean passage from India to Britain. Equally astonishing were the powers of the cow wastes: the stool, spread in a thin layer across the floor of a home and allowed to dry, formed a powdery 'carpet' on which no fly or unwanted pest would land, while the cow's urine was a cure for various dangerous diseases. Though they were not induced to acknowledge it, India's new rulers found some of her ancient religious beliefs suprisingly scientific. It would have been no surprise to an enlightened thinker like Albert Einstein, who once remarked, "Science without religion is lame, religion without science is blind" (26).

Just how do scientific explanations compare to religious explanations? Are these conflicting approaches to the same subject matter, or complementary approaches to distinct subject matters? Can scientific explanations and religious beliefs be reconciled?

Defining and distinguishing branches of intellectual activity such as science and religion falls in the realm of philosophy. Intellectual disciplines can be analyzed according to certain general features: their *objects, aims,* and *methods* (Peterson et al. 198). When there is a similarity in the evaluation of religion and science according to these three, the potential for conflict arises.

A typical example of such conflict is biological evolution versus the biblical conception of creation. It appears that the supporters of both, if speaking about the same objects—namely the world and universe we live in—are also suggesting aims for their explanations of how the object under discussion came into existence. Certainly their explanations differ, as do their methods of reaching their conclusions. Biblical evolutionists cite various proof texts from the Genesis creation account, while evolutionists use empirical hypotheses backed by ongoing research. Observing the conflict, some creationists have also adopted the scientific method to validate their claims. This, however, has not spared them from being branded "false scientists" by evolutionists. Nicholas Wolterstorff has explained that fundamentalists use their theological claims as "control beliefs" (199). Evolutionary theory is then evaluated according to such 'controls' and accepted or rejected insofar as it supports or fails to support the theological norms.

Evolutionary naturalism, as propounded by such men as Charles Darwin and Julian Huxley, responded to the conflict between science and religion by condemning biblical authority and natural theology altogether (200). With the support of *philosophical naturalism,* which holds that matter alone is real, the evolutionary naturalists created a world-view of humanity facing an essentially hostile, purposeless universe. Science alone could improve human destiny and provide a meaningful explanation for existence to replace the failure of theology and metaphysics.

Evolutionary naturalism has been debunked by creationists and others who blame its conclusions for, among other things, a wide range of dehumanizing influences. Taking a hint from this critique, it could be suggested that evolutionists might do well to find a means to accommodate theological beliefs, just as creationists would do well not to insist that science adjust its established findings to adhere to certain overly simplistic scriptural formulas.

One way to ensure that the gap between the two is not widened is to demonstrate that science and religion function in entirely separate spheres. If it can be established that they differ markedly in terms of their objects, methods, and aims—that they are *compartmentalized*—then the conflict can be avoided.

The theological position of *neo-orthodoxy* and the philosophical conception of *existentialism* are quite similar in maintaining a distinct contrast between science and religion (201). The Protestant theologian Karl Barth has explained how science and religion differ in terms of objects, methodology, and aims. Christianity deals with God's self-revelation in Christ whereas science deals with the natural world. In terms of methodology, God can be known only if he chooses to reveal himself to us, whereas our understanding of nature depends upon the proper use of our reason. The aims of the two are as radically distinct: the religionist desires an encounter with God, while the scientist seeks an understanding of the patterns of the empirical world. Establishing fundamental differences in terms of objects, methods, and aims enables neo-orthodoxy to eliminate what would ordinarily be the conflict between science and religion.

Existentialism is equally committed to establishing this difference. The theistic existentialists (and their atheistic counterparts) trace their origin to the nineteenth-century work of Soren Kierkegaard (201). Science, they say, is impersonal and objective, while religion is deeply personal and subjective. The objects of science are material things, whereas the objects of religion are personal and moral realities. The Jewish theologian Martin Buber expresses this distinction: "I-it" characterizes the person-object relationship, "I-Thou" the relationship between the believer and God. The believer seeks meaningful reciprocity with God, a goal quite contrary to the scientist's clinical, detached study. Such vastly disparate objects and aims obviously necessitate entirely different methodologies. Neo-orthodoxy and existentialism are in this regard *fideistic* in maintaining that faith is not subject to rational scrutiny. For them, the endeavors of religion and science are separately compartmentalized with no possible overlapping.

According to twentieth-century *positivism*, a view already considered in a previous chapter, only empirical objects provide points of reference for meaningful language. Nonempirical objects (e.g., God and the soul) are cognitively meaningless. Science, not religion, is rational and objective and therefore capable of yielding genuine knowledge. Though the positivist conclusion is an affront to theistic existentialism, their implications (at least in terms of our interest here) are strangely similar: compartmentalizing religion and science rules out the possibility of conflict.

Unlike the positivists, *ordinary language* analysts, following the lead of Wittgenstein, see relevancy in all approaches—the scientific, religious, etc. (202). Each is a viable "language-game" with its own categories and logic. Ordinary language philosophers do not care to judge the truth of a particular discipline's claim as much as to study its functions. Scientific language aims at prediction and control, while theological language describes worship and comfort. Ordinary language philosophy is as different from positivism as the latter is from theistic existentialism. Yet, as in the latter two cases, by demonstrating that science and religion are different 'languages,' there is no possibility of interaction or conflict.

Thus far we have assessed the dialectic of science and religion in conflict and compartmentalization. Another view seeks to find some compatibility between the two, treating theological claims as though they are scientific hypotheses or actually assimilating them into large-scale hypotheses. George Schlesinger, for instance, advocates subjecting the factual implications of religious claims to the scientific method (202). Whether or not this is productive and what exactly the results of such investigation indicate is debatable. This type of approach may leave us wondering whether more traditional methods of evaluating theology might not be more appropriate. *Process philosophy* is another approach which aims at establishing a viable connection between religion and science (203). Rather than merely subjecting theological claims to scientific-style scrutiny, the process method, following the lead of Alfred North Whitehead, proposes a comprehensive world-view which draws data from both religious and scientific experience.

Donald MacKay, a British philosopher in science, has proposed a further interesting alternative. He suggests that the relationship of science and theology is one of *complementarity*. Though they attempt to give different kinds of explanations using different methods and aims, the objects they seek to explain are the same. "Complementarity here means that both scientific and theological explanations of the same event can be true and complete at their own levels. But the methods and aims of the two enterprises differ markedly" (203). MacKay's ideas hark back to those of Charles Colson and Karl Hein. He believes that the job of science is to seek the *causes* of events, whereas theology aims to deliver the *meaning* of events. Though neither explanation is dependent on the other, we require both for a more complete understanding.

MacKay clarifies the meaning of the term *complementarity*, distinguishing it from *supplementarity*. On one hand, when constructing a building there would be many drawings from various perspectives that could be considered supplementary descriptions of the same thing. On the other hand, complementarity "is a relationship among descriptions or explanations that involve differences in *viewpoint* . . . Complementarity in this sense characterizes the different ways an artist, a poet, or an astronomer might view a sunset from their respective conceptual frameworks, creating different levels of understanding" (204). How this relates to the previously discussed conflict and compartmentalized views of science and religion is explained succinctly by MacKay:

> "In the context of science and theology, it (complementarity) offers an alternative both to the view that makes all divine activity supplementary to the (presumed incomplete) chain mesh of scientifically describable cause and effect ('God in the gaps'), and to the 'watertight compartment' theory that religious and scientific statements are logically independent." (204)

Thus, complementarity allows for a scientific and theological explanation of the same event, though each is exclusive and exhaustive. MacKay's thought would, for example, accommodate a scientific explanation of the universe while simultaneously allowing the creationist viewpoint as well. Following his approach, advocates of either would not feel intimidated by the other's conception. Scientists could maintain their "big bang" or "steady state" scenarios, while theists could continue to insist on God's guiding hand. The subject of one discipline cannot be addressed by the method of the other.

There is obvious value to MacKay's concept. Religion would not be subjected to an incompatible scientific evaluation, nor would science be forced to fit rigid theological prescriptions. Yet MacKay's solution brings with it certain inherent problems. Do the ramifications of certain scientific investigations not perhaps conflict with basic theological claims? Is human freedom, for example, undermined by scientific determinism? An instance in point is MacKay's own investigation of the workings of the brain evaluated as a mechanistic system. Seeing that the brain functions in a similarly determined pattern as the movements of a clock may conflict with the Christian theological conception of the human as a free and responsible moral agent. MacKay defends his position by explaining that the mechanistic hypothesis is merely a "working assumption," while theology views freedom as an aspect of "moral and spiritual reality" (205). The problem with MacKay's response is that it suggests that the scientific approach does not attempt to actually depict reality. Certainly, science does attempt to do so, and MacKay himself is a committed scientist. Hence, his mechanistic hypothesis is not a mere viewing of the brain, but must be seen as providing insight into reality. This brings religion and science into potential conflict.

The issue of freedom and determinism is only one case that must be worked out for the theory of complementarity to stand. Another is whether just any two explanations can be compatible. And, how can we be certain in advance that no scientific and religious claims concerning the same event will never conflict? MacKay's proposition may be overly strong. Peterson et al. voice the obvious doubt that a solution which allows for totally different methodologies to explain the *same* objects can be so strongly guaranteed (206). It would seem that the claims of religion and science need to be evaluated on a case-by-case basis. An overriding consideration is the value of importance assigned to either the religious or scientific viewpoint as "knowledge-seeking" or "belief-forming" practices. What if the two systems define a particular situation in conflicting ways? How much conflict is permissible for them still to be considered complementary? It has also been pointed out that each discipline borrows elements from the other while formulating its respective systems. Scientists borrow hunches, metaphors, and intuitions from the general cultural, religiously influenced environment, while theologians borrow elements from their contemporary culture as well (207). Yet MacKay would argue that complementarity describes more than such superficial borrowing; it actually pertains to their broader, underlying world-views.

Up until this point we have been evaluating the relationship between religion and science. Just as there are distinctive religious traditions with disparate approaches to fundamental issues, science also has its clearly distinctive approaches. In particular, there is a long-standing debate as to whether the "social" sciences (e.g., psychology and sociology) have unique characteristics which distinguish them from the "natural" sciences (e.g., physics, chemistry, and biology) (208). Those who advocate the distinction point out that the social (often called "human") sciences are largely concerned with humans, and as such require a special method of study. Studies of human behavior require "sympathetic understanding," something not easily provided by the classic scientific methods. Wilhelm Dilthey points out that human reason and intentions require the kind of empathetic understanding impossible to find in the natural sciences.

Opponents to this view argue that all the sciences share a common methodology, but that the relatively younger social sciences need to work further to adapt this traditional methodology for their studies. B. F. Skinner insists that the cause-effect analysis so basic to all sciences is equally applicable when studying human behavior, for causes operate in the human realm as extensively as they do amongst the lower animals. But the most persuasive arguments for the unity of the sciences "revolve around the thesis that they share the same *logic* of justification (for the validation of theories)" (208).

Since our primary interest here is the relationship between science and religion, let us assume that there are two distinct branches of science. What analogies may then be drawn between the social sciences and theology? Certainly these analogies will center around what it means to explain the actions of "rational agents" in terms of reasons and intentions. Richard Swinburne's view of the distinction between scientific explanation and personal explanation is that "[s]cientific explanation focuses on the powers and liabilities inherent in impersonal physical objects, while personal explanation focuses on the intentions of rational, personal agents" (209). The implication is that the distinction Swinburne draws between science and religion closely parallels the two broad divisions of science. Since many religions posit a relationship between humans and the divine, human behavior may inform us of divine behavioral patterns. Could the methodologies employed by the human sciences not be helpful in revealing aspects of the Divine?

The possibility that science may be employed as an aid in theological inquiry is recognized in the Vedic tradition. Religion and science are not opposed, as biologist T.D. Singh, a disciple of A. C. Bhaktivedanta Swami Prabhupada, explains in "Vedantic Views on Evolution," an essay in *Synthesis of Science and Religion*:

> In Vedanta there has always been harmony between science and religion because their domains are clearly defined and understood. Science deals with *apara vidya*, or material knowledge; true religion deals with *para vidya*, spiritual knowledge. Knowledge of one's body and its components, atoms, and molecules is *apara vidya*; knowledge of the conscious living being (*the atma*), transcendental life, and God is *para vidya*. A *para vidya* can be experienced through sensory perceptions, but *para vidya* is experienced through the discipline of yoga and the science of meditation. A *para vidya* indicates the existence of *para vidya*. Srimad Bhagavatam states that *parasya drsyate dharmo hy aparasmin samanvayat* (3.26.49): "Since the cause exists certainly in its effect as well, the characteristics of the former are observed in the latter." This is a synthetic principle of *Vedanta*. (97)

Singh's explanation of the synthetic view in Vedanta is a particularly interesting alternative to MacKay's *complementarity* thesis. Whereas for MacKay science and theology differ in methods and aims but agree in the objects of study, in Singh's evaluation, the methods and objects differ, but the aim is one. The Vedas often join science and theology by committing them to a common aim. The highly admired Vedic system of *sankhya*[1] seeks to distinguish the soul, a spiritual particle, from the material elements by a minute analysis of the element's specific qualities. The intention is to establish the primacy of the soul and, hence, the relative importance of self realization as opposed to temporal pleasure. But by no means is sense pleasure or material existence denied; rather the Vedic system attempts to harness the material energy to achieve a transcendental goal. True, the senses, and for that matter, material life are temporary; but as material existence is the field of activity for the embodied soul, it is of the utmost importance. Any negative ascriptions applied to the material energy are only meant to serve as reminders that it is not the soul's final resting place.

That Vedic authorities were not disinterested in material existence is attested to by the expertise of Indian mathematicians and astronomers, a fact not only appreciated by the peoples of other ancient cultures but well-documented in modern times as well. Delineations by Vedic thinkers anticipated many later Western 'discoveries' in both the natural and social sciences. Fields as diverse as medicine (*ayur veda*), weaponry (*dhanur veda*), city planning (*silpa shastra*), calculations of time (*kala-vichara*), and social organization (*dharma shastra*), to name but a few, indicate a sophisticated culture without any ancient parallel. The Vedas are encyclopedic in their sweep of all branches of knowledge. Significantly, their focus is often on *this* world, not the world beyond, for that *other* world would remain forever beyond reach if the quality of life in this world were neglected. Thus, Vedic authorities took great pains to refine their knowledge of all the sciences with a view to speeding the human journey onward to its final destination.

One therefore wishes that the authors of *Reason and Religious*

---

[1] I am speaking here of the theistic *sankhya* of Devahuti Kapila as opposed to the atheistic *sankhya* by another Kapila.

Belief were not so poorly informed that they would write:

> . . . of the relatively underdeveloped state of science in other ancient
> and premodern cultures. For example, modern science, which advances
> through commerce with the empirical realm, could not take root in
> Hindu culture, where this realm is conceived to be either illusory or
> unreal, and where the chief goal is release from this world, trapped as
> it is in an endless cycle of birth-death-rebirth. (213)

It appears that Peterson et al. are only aware of monistic Vedanta
with its utter pessimistic view of this world. The monotheistic
Vedantists, as has just been demonstrated, approach this world
with enthusiasm. They see matter as an energy of God and
therefore do not reject it; instead they engage matter in the service
of God. Still, one wonders how the authors could have ignored
the scientific achievements of Vedic civilization which are so
patent that they hardly require enumeration. Such uninformed
statements appear to smack of geographical and theological
prejudice. If the Vedic view perceives the world as "unreal," why
have the Vedas and their followers delved with such an intense
investigatory nature into each and every nuance of material
existence? Can the authors show any close comparison directly
within the Judeo-Christian tradition? Rather, it could be posited,
it is specifically because of the absence of thorough investigation
of things material in the Judeo-Christian scriptures that the
disciplines of material science have been ultimately forfeited to
the hands of nonreligious materialists.

The Vedanta never divorced science from religion as has
happened in the Judeo-Christian world. There was no necessity
for such a split. The God of the Vedas created the universes by
his own volition, out of loving compassion for his children, who
chose also of their own volition to separate themselves from him.
Because he is all-good, and because these universes emanate from
him, they must also be good. Whatever the authors have said of
the Judeo-Christian God could easily have been applied to the

God of the Vedas. To quote Michael Foster:

> "A world which is created by the Christian God will be both
> contingent and orderly. It will embody regularities and patterns, since
> its Maker is rational, but the particular regularities and patterns which
> it will embody cannot be predicted *a priori*, since he is free; they can
> be discovered only by examination. The world, as Christian theism
> conceives, is thus an ideal field for the application of scientific method,
> with its twin techniques of observation and experiment." (211)

The Vedic theologian will have no problem with Foster's
opening remarks regarding the orderliness of the Creator's work.
It is the second half of Foster's statement that will cause
disagreement. God's 'freedom' does not automatically rule out
the possibility of *a priori* 'prediction.' A truly free God may, if
he so desires, elaborately explain the past, present, or future. To
deny God this right is to limit God. If God so chooses to explain
the particular regularities and patterns which the world will
embody, then the role of science is no longer *discovery* but
confirmation. The "application of the scientific method, with its
twin techniques of observation and experiment" will then be used
to confirm, rather than discover anew, what God has revealed.

It may be argued that the impetus for scientific investigation
will be diminished if the conclusions of such investigation are
already accepted truths from the start. This is not necessarily so.
Rather, scientific efforts would be directed to demonstrate the
truth of Vedic formulas by practical creations meant for human
benefit. Many 'modern' discoveries and inventions are indicated
in Vedic texts and were utilized by Vedic practitioners thousands
of years ago. Unfortunately, the scientific ability to demonstrate
the truth of these Vedic statements is now lost, for it is a subtle
science requiring a degree of spiritual advancement rarely found
in the present age.

Though Peterson et al. may argue that the presuppositions
about nature and the knowledge of nature found in the Judeo-

Christian world-view were particularly conducive to the advancement of science, it could be equally argued that it was specifically the *lack* of substantive information regarding nature within the tradition's foundational scriptures that forced thinkers to observe, hypothesize, and experiment for themselves. It is not our intention here to belittle one religious tradition to favor another. Rather, we subscribe to the view that there is one Supreme God who is worshipped within a multiplicity of religious traditions. If it be found that the Vedic tradition more perfectly melded religion and science than did the Judeo-Christian conception, it is no way a loss to the latter, for both traditions are but sub-sets of divine revelation.

We shall conclude by calling upon another esteemed disciple of Prabhupada, theologian William Deadwyler:

> The Sanskrit word *veda* means "knowledge," but modern people categorize the *Vedas*—India's ancient books of knowledge—as "scripture," having to do with religion as opposed to knowledge and science. This opposition between religion and science, however, is a modern phenomenon, a product of the historical process of secularization. We are now beginning to realize that this split between religion and science is a critical problem—even *the* critical problem—for humanity, and perhaps the *Vedas* themselves, coming from a culture that antedated such divided consciousness, can give us help in our search for a renewed wholeness.

> I think those of us gathered here to explore possibilities for the synthesis of science and religion recognize that the present estrangement between them constitutes a critical problem for the modern world. Indeed, this problem, in various guises, can be seen as the central dilemma of Western culture since the Renaissance. Science, sundered from religion, is blind, unable to guide human life according to ultimate ends; religion, sundered from science, is lame, incapable of conveying its vision into the thick of our actual commerce with the world. The religion and science of modernity, conceived in mutual disjunction, embodied in separate institutions, and grown to conscious

self-definition over against one another, have both emerged historically as handicapped and unwholesome caricatures of the whole they ought to be—the single human enterprise we may call either a truly religious science or a truly scientific religion. (366-8)

Religious Pluralism:

How Can We Understand Religious Diversity?

An ancient hermetic dictum states, "as above, so below." Projecting this truism onto the field of religious diversity, are we to understand that such diversity also exists "above"? In that transcendent world of God, if ever we have entry, shall we expect to meet Muslims, Christians, Jews, Buddhists and Hindus? And if so, would they bear the same unique characteristics of faith they manifest in this world? As empirical information of the world "above" is difficult to obtain, we should look for our answer from the religions themselves. But what an array of responses we shall meet! We shall be tossed and tumbled upon the waves of religious diversity, caught in the cross-currents of denominational competition, to be thrown, battered and bruised, upon the shore of confusion. Our experience with multi-religionism will have served one purpose at least: it will strengthen our hope, if we have any left, that the situation above may be less bewildering. But for now we will have to disentangle ourselves from the mass of seaweed, massage our aches and pains, and, looking over the choppy waters, ponder our present options. Should we follow the *exclusivist* approach of a particular denomination? Perhaps either the *pluralist* or *inclusivist* approach to religious diversity would be a better option.

Our task is not to analyze how an advocate of one religion

should approach an advocate of another; rather, we wish to know how "one should approach *what* another person advocates" (Peterson et al. 221). The first is a moral question, the latter a study of the method and grounds for the particular belief with reference to its limits and validity. To evaluate a person's truth-claims is not necessarily the same as evaluating the person. We can be tolerant of all without necessarily accepting what each believes. Or, as A.C. Bhaktivedanta Swami Prabhupada once stated, "criticize the belief, not the believer." This will avoid the exclusivist fanaticism of the jihads, crusades, inquisitions, and pogroms, as well as, at the opposite side of the spectrum, militant atheism. (Some would suggest that modern atheistic humanism is more deadly than any crusade of the past.)

John Hick offers three approaches to religious diversity (221). A religion is *exclusivist* when it claims that its teachings are the sole means to attain salvation or whatever else its goals may be. Other religions may share certain of its truth claims, but its claims alone are exclusively true. This being so, once one finds that true religion, it would be foolish to search elsewhere.

Protestant theologian Karl Barth presents this exclusivist doctrine of salvation through Jesus Christ (222). For Barth, the revelation of God comes exclusively through the medium of Jesus. Religion, however, is a human endeavor which often interferes with such revelation. Barth does not see Christianity as a superior religion; rather, it is the *facilitator* of the true religion, namely, the revelation of Jesus Christ. This doctrine is by no means unique; other religious proponents have championed with equal fervor the uniqueness of their founder and the founder's teachings.

Of course, Barth's presupposition that there is only one revelation can be questioned. Certainly an infinite God is capable of communicating in different ways according to time, place, and circumstance. Can we really say that members of other religions cannot achieve perfection merely for failing to embrace the teachings or the founding person of a particular religious faith? What if we see total transformation in the character and lives of the advocates of other religions? Are we automatically to rule out that such change may have a divine cause? Certainly we cannot judge one exclusivist religion's claims of superiority over another solely on the basis of its adherents' moral character since there are morally upright as well as spiritually advanced persons in every other exclusivist religion as well.

Instead of favoring one religion over all others, a wiser path may be to accept that the divine can be revealed through a multiplicity of religions. Scriptures, the saintly behavior of its adherents, and time-tested traditions are certifications for the reliability of a religion's truth-claims. This is *pluralism*, the form of religious diversity Hick himself favors.

The concept raises immediate questions. How can systems which sometimes explain God in totally conflicting ways be simultaneously true? Hick responds by distinguishing Reality as it is in itself (the *noumena*) and Reality as it is humanly and culturally experienced (the *phenomena*) (224). The particular life-experience of each human will naturally color his or her interpretation. The classic example of the blind men who examined different parts of an elephant's body and drew totally disparate conclusions as to the identity of the elephant, clearly demonstrates that our individual and cultural limitations limit our religious perspectives. Reality is infinite and cannot be described completely by any individual or system; hence, religious pluralism.

How does Hick respond to exclusivist claims? Hick denies any orthodox view of exclusive incarnation. Rather, he allows that the Divine can manifest through all individuals by transforming their lives. Jesus (and other saintly personalities) are examples of such Reality-centered transformation. Hick cautions against too strong an emphasis on doctrines or histories; these are but human attempts to explain the Divine. They are valuable to the degree that they encourage personal transformation, but are not intrinsically significant. If religions are viewed simply as life-transforming methods, what matters is not the difference in methodology as much as the commonality in results. Peterson et al. correctly assess Hick's position: "Thus, exactly what one believes is not all that important; it is a mythic projection of one's own experience, culture, and conceptual categories on Reality" (225).

It would seem that Hick's response to religious diversity is one of concern more for morality than epistemology. Are we actually to ignore the truth-claims about Reality which religions traditionally make? Some pluralists respond that truth is simply how Reality appears at a particular time and place, and in a particular historical perspective (226). Other pluralists say that religion simply makes truth-claims about Reality understood phenomenally. Pluralists also at times state that religious language and concepts are used to promote achievement of the ultimate Reality, unlike scientific language which is used to verify our ordinary experiences.

All of this is not to say that there is no way of rationally scrutinizing religious systems. Hick argues that internal consistency and experiential adequacy are the appropriate means of judgment. But this only explains the relevancy of particular statements *within* a system; it gives no indication of the overall truth of Reality viewed from *without*. Also, experiential adequacy is based on the same cultural and personal subjectivity upon which religious claims are said to be based. Furthermore, by imposing, for example, logical consistency, how will Hick accommodate Zen Buddhists who maintain that such intellectual endeavor is but a symptom of human conditioning to be transcended?

It would seem that Hick's emphasis on the person-relative view of Reality can easily lead to skepticism. One could argue, using the elephant analogy, that not only are the individual reports incomplete, but if everything is simply a subjective personal assessment, perhaps there is no elephant at all! Overemphasis on the subjective at the expense of clear relationships between religious propositions and the Reality they are said to describe has led "some pluralists to admit atheistic Marxism and naturalistic humanism into the camp of religions alongside and on equal footing with theism" (227). This alone underscores the serious problems besetting the pluralist approach. "If we have no clear concept of God, if we are left with nothing to be said about God or the Ultimate as it is in itself, our religious belief more closely approximates unbelief and becomes relatively indistinguishable from atheism" (227). As Peter Geach has argued, "worship" is an intentional verb. Our worship is directed towards someone, and it does matter to whom this worship is directed.

If we accept the pluralist view that there are many varied possibilities of religious and life-transforming experiences, and that God can reveal himself in a variety of ways, while at the same time we affirm the need to assess the truth or falsity of truth-claims about reality, we have what Hick terms *religious inclusivism* (228). However, inclusivists assert that the absolute truth can be known truly *in only one religion*. In this sense they agree with exclusivists; yet, in that they allow that God can be encountered and his grace manifested in various diverse religions, they agree with pluralists. Thus, inclusivism extends beyond the exclusivist reach by acknowledging that other religions may share some of the truth-claims of the one true religion and thus also be capable of advancing their adherents.

The Catholic theologian Karl Rahner postulates that persons are offered salvation by the occurrence of a particular event of salvational quality. Specifically, Christianity is the absolute religion which alone can deliver the true way of salvation. However, God can make the benefit of Jesus's atonement available to all persons, even to those who have never heard of Jesus or accepted him as their savior. Thus, those outside of Christianity can also experience transformation and be reconciled to God. An analogous scenario is presented to make the point clear. A large number of poor in a particular town have no way of paying their creditors. A wealthy matron from another town hears of their plight and decides to deposit a large sum on their behalf with their town's bank. Though the poor know nothing of her or of her charity, her objective act of depositing on their behalf allows them to withdraw the needed funds to absolve their debts.

Rahner notes that although Christianity has its historical beginnings with Jesus's birth, it has a prehistory as well. Israelites and other faithful living before Christ's birth are, according to the New Testament, saved subjectively by their faith and objectively by the still-future obedience of Christ. There are many even today who are in a similar position, having never heard the Christian gospel. Since God desires that all persons be saved, it is reasonable to think that God would apply the same grace to these new persons as he did to the Israelites and others of old. Rahner calls such fortunate persons *anonymous Christians* (229).

Should such persons continue to adhere to their own faith? Rahner admits that religion is not simply an internal affair but is also embodied in the institutions—social, cultural and otherwise—of the particular religion. The true religion best facilitates the individual's relationship with God. Still, God's grace can be made available even if one follows another religion, just as pre-Christian Judaism sufficiently nourished its believers. This thinking could give equal justification to other, non-Christian inclusivists. Each religion could hold itself to be the true religion while acknowledging the potential validity of other religions' beliefs proportionate to the degree of agreement with their belief systems.

But why call believers anonymous Christians, or anonymous Hindus, if they have never even heard of the particular religion? Why this attempt at conversion? Why not simply allow them to follow the religion of their own persuasion? Rahner's response is that things being equal, a Christian has a better chance of salvation than does an anonymous Christian (230). Other inclusivists would go further by stating that it does, in fact, count that persons know the true basis of their salvation, because liberation comes through knowledge of the truth.

Of course, the real question raised by the inclusivist view is how to determine which is the true religion. Are we to accept the truth-claims of Christianity, or Islam, or any other? And on what basis? Shall we judge the relative merit of religious founders or of their respective teachings? For example, is the moral life of Jesus superior to that of the Buddha? Or, are we instead to assess the historical tradition which grew from these founders' teachings? Certainly this type of exercise would be fraught with obvious difficulties, for no religion can boast of an immaculate history.

Perhaps we should try to find some criteria by which we can evaluate the religious systems themselves. Can we, for example, subject the truth-claims to rational evaluation? We can use logic, experience, and other such methods to judge the truth or falsity of a particular belief. Beyond this, we could try to make comparative evaluations of the religions themselves. Keith Yandell and others have tried to formulate objective criteria (230). Yet one wonders if these will provide a sufficient basis for judgment. After all, religions are not simply isolated objective statements of beliefs, but complex social systems grown within a culture, whose characteristics would also need to be taken into account and subjected to evaluation. Furthermore, religions historically undergo transformation themselves until hundreds of years later they may differ greatly from the founders' original conception. On what grounds, or at what time in history are they to be judged? Peterson et al. even opine that no religion can get back to and believe in exactly what the original founders believed and practiced. Add to this the fact that religion means something different to each of its adherents. Which adherent's conception are we to judge?

In India, a long history of religious tolerance bespeaks of a broad-minded approach which deserves our thoughtful consideration. The puzzle of religious diversity has been carefully analyzed by two eminent theologians of the Vaishnava Hindu tradition. Bhaktivinode Thakura (1838-1914) and A. C. Bhaktivedanta Swami Prabhupada (1896-1977) had reason to respond to the diverse religious panorama of their times. As the modern representatives of an ancient preceptorial line of teachers, they encountered all the major world religions and eloquently expressed in the English language their conclusions regarding the question of religious diversity. Their viewpoint is an ideal form of inclusivism.

Bhaktivinode Thakura was educated in British India and rose in the Government's service to the position of High Court Magistrate of Puri. Hence, he had numerous occasions to meet persons of varied social, cultural, and religious backgrounds. Vastly learned and well read, and a prolific writer, he addressed the subject of religious diversity in a number of his works. In *The Bhagavata: Its Philosophy, Its Ethics, and Its Theology*, he reconciles intellectual diversity:

> Subjects of philosophy and theology are like the peaks of large, towering and inaccessible mountains standing in the midst of our planet inviting attention and investigation. Thinkers and men of deep speculation take their observations through the instruments of reason and consciousness. But they take their stand on different points when they carry on their work. These points are positions chalked out by the circumstances of their social and philosophical life, different as they are in the different parts of the world. Plato looked at the peak of the Spiritual question from the West and Vyasa made the observation from the East; so Confucius did it from further East, and Schlegel, Spinoza, Kant and Goethe from further West. These observations were made at different times and by different means, but the conclusion is all the same in as much as the object of observation was one and the same. They all searched after the Great Spirit, the unconditioned Soul of the Universe. They could not but get an insight into it. Their words and expressions are different, but their import is

the same. They tried to find out the absolute religion and their labours were crowned with success, for God gives all that He has to His children if they want to have it. (7-8)

The Thakura's generous appreciation for philosophy as well as religion was based on his contention that each is searching in its own way for an understanding of the highest truth. He does not gloss over the philosophical and theological differences but, as will be seen, considers them secondary, much as the basic human nature is the same everywhere, but the secondary human traits may vary. This he explains in a summary study of Sri Chaitanya's teachings entitled *Shri Chaitanya Shikshamritam*:

> Though the main human nature is the same, yet no two human beings will be found in the world whose secondary natures will be quite the same between themselves. How will men born in different countries be of the same nature, when two brothers of the same mother are different in appearance and nature, never the same in all respects? The waters, atmospheres, mountain systems, sylvan orders, food products and materials for clothings are all different in the different countries. Due to it the bodily structures, complexions, usages, clothings and food-articles of men born in them have become different in accordance with the difference in their acquired natures compatible with the respective environments. The mental conditions, too, become similarly different in particular countries. And the inclinations towards God as included therein though the same principally, become different along with the differences in their languages, clothings, edibles, temperaments, etc. When considered with an impartial view of the affairs, there is no harm caused by these secondary differences. There is nothing wrong at the time of fruition, if there is unity in respect of the principal object of worship. (6)

The differences in human nature, then, are traced to social, cultural, and geographical causes. These influences account for many of the differences observed in various religions regarding "(i) the acharyas or preceptors, (ii) the mental predilection and concepts of worshipers, (iii) the systems of worship, (iv) the conceptions and conventional actions concerning the object of worship, and (v) the names and words according to linguistic differences" (*Shri Chaitanya Shikshamritam* 7). These differences are of secondary importance compared to the primary issue of "the principle object of worship." This necessitates examining each religion's specific truth-claims.

But the Thakura does not approve of the exclusivist view of any religion as holding itself superior to another on account of the speciality of its founder. "It is not proper to insistently propagate the controversial superiority of the teachings of the acharyas [great teachers] of one's own country over those of all the other countries," he writes, "though one may, should, cherish such a belief in order to acquire steadiness in the faith of one's own. No good can be effected to the world by such quarrels" (7). Here, he recognizes that the psychology of the believer requires that he or she hold the religion's founder to be superior to all others in order to strengthen his or her own faith. Yet he cautions against such sectarianism. Hindu religion was often deprecated by the British rulers, and European indologists were not always objective in their assessment of Indian religion. In *The Bhagavata*, Bhaktivinode Thakura advises critics to be sympathetic:

> The true critic is a generous judge, void of prejudices and party-spirit. One who is at heart the follower of Mohammed will certainly find the doctrines of the New Testament to be a forgery by the fallen angel. A Trinitarian Christian, on the other hand, will denounce the precepts of Mohammed as those of an ambitious reformer. The reason simply is that the critic should be of the same disposition of mind as that of the author, whose merits he is required to judge. Thoughts have different ways. One who is trained up in thoughts of the Unitarian Society or of that of the *Vedant* of the Benares School, will scarcely find piety in the faith of the Vaishnavas. An ignorant Vaishnava, on the other hand, whose business is only to beg from door to door in the name of Nityananda will find no piety in a Christian. This is because the Vaishnava does not think in the way in which the Christian thinks of his own religion. It may be that both the Christian and the

Vaishnava will utter the same sentiment, but they will never stop their fight with each other only because they have arrived at their common conclusion through different ways of thoughts. Thus a great deal of ungenerousness enters into the arguments of the pious Christians when they pass their imperfect opinion on the religion of the Vaishnavas. (6-7)

The Thakura gives a practical suggestion on how the members of each religion should view the practices of others. His advice reads like a modern-day interfaith handbook:

When we may have an occasion to be present at the place of worship of other religionists at the time of their worship, we should be staying there in a respectful mood contemplating thus: "Here is being worshipped my adorable Highest Entity (God in a different form from that of mine). Due to my practice of a different kind, I cannot thoroughly comprehend this system of theirs; but seeing it, I am feeling a greater attachment for my own system. The Highest Entity (i.e., God) is not more than one. I bow down with prostration before His emblem as I see here and I offer my prayer to my Lord Who has adopted this different emblem that He may increase my love towards Him in the form as acceptable for me. (*Shri Chaitanya Shikshamritam* 8-9)

It is unlikely that this pluralistic view will lead to the kind of skepticism which Hick's ideas may generate. Bhaktivinode Thakura is not merely advocating an all-inclusive accommodation. Yet Peterson et al.'s assessment that for Hick belief is simply a "projection of one's own experience, culture, and conceptual categories on reality" may, in light of what has been said above, seem equally applicable. But from all of the Thakura's writings we know that he placed the highest value on correctly assessing a religion's truth-claims. For a religion to be a religion, it must have a "principle object of worship." He would insist, as does Geach, that "our worship is directed toward someone, and it does matter to whom this worship is directed" (227). This is the common bond that cements all religions. It is also the distinction which separates theism from non-theism. As liberal as the Thakura was, he would not compromise with atheism in any of its moral disguises. Thus:

> The religions in which there prevail the evils like atheism, skepticism, materialism, no-soulism like epicurianism, pantheism, polytheism and nondistinct monism—should not be regarded as the devotees of God. They should be known as counterreligions, pseudo religions and false religions. Their followers are really unfortunate. Jivas [living beings] should be, as far as practicable, protected against those evils. Pure love is the eternal virtue of jivas. Even though the five kinds of difference as said above are noticeable, that religion is true religion in which the attainment of pure love of God is the object aimed at. It is improper to quarrel over extraneous differences. If the aim of a religion is pure love, then all the other circumstances are to be looked upon as proper. The doctrines of atheism, etc., as cited above, are unnatural and antagonistic to love. (*Shri Chaitanya Shikshamritam* 9)

But is this some sort of "group" exclusivism? Though apparently pluralistic, the Thakura appears to be a veiled exclusivist. This is certainly not the case. While Hick's pluralism is achieved, "not only at the extremely high price of skepticism, but in disregard of what believers think they are doing" (227), Bhaktivinode Thakura is able to base his views on strong and clearly defined belief-claims that are at the same time truly nonsectarian. They hinge on the Vedic definition of religion, or more precisely, *sanatana-dharma*. To understand this concept we will now take the help of his great grand-disciple, the founder of the Hare Krishna movement.

When A. C. Bhaktivedanta Swami Prabhupada arrived in the West, he had to introduce what appeared to be a 'foreign' religion. The Vedas were in Sanskrit, the Deity Krishna apparently a Hindu god. Westerners viewed his mission with suspicion. Was his mission merely the latest in the long multi-religious history of proselytizing attempts? He knew this to be the primary question in the public's mind and therefore he chose to address it directly in his Introduction to the *Bhagavad-gita As It Is*, the "Hindu Bible":

Man professes to belong to a particular type of faith with reference to particular time and circumstance and thus claims to be a Hindu, Muslim, Christian, Buddhist or an adherent of any other sect. Such designations are non-*sanatana-dharma*. A Hindu may change his faith to become a Muslim, or a Muslim may change his faith to become a Hindu, or a Christian may change his faith and so on. But in all circumstances the change of religious faith does not affect the eternal occupation of rendering service to others. The Hindu, Muslim or Christian in all circumstances is servant to someone. Thus, to profess a particular type of faith is not to profess one's *sanatana-dharma*. The rendering of service is *sanatana-dharma*.

Therefore, *sanatana-dharma* does not refer to any sectarian process of religion. It is the eternal function of the eternal living entities in relationship with the eternal Supreme Lord. *Sanatana-dharma* refers, as stated previously, to the eternal occupation of the living entity. Sripada Ramanujacarya has explained the word *sanatana* as "that which has neither beginning nor end," so when we speak of *sanatana-dharma*, we must take it for granted on the authority of Sripada Ramanujacarya that it has neither beginning nor end.

The English word *religion* is a little different from *sanatana-dharma*. *Religion* conveys the idea of faith, and faith may change. One may have faith in a particular process, and he may change this faith and adopt another, but *sanatana-dharma* refers to that activity which cannot be changed. For instance, liquidity cannot be taken from water, nor can heat be taken from fire. Similarly, the eternal function of the eternal living entity cannot be taken from the living entity. *Sanatana-dharma* is eternally integral with the living entity. When we speak of *sanatana-dharma*, therefore, we must take it for granted on the authority of Sripada Ramanujacarya that it has neither beginning nor end. That which has neither end nor beginning must not be sectarian, for it cannot be limited by any boundaries. Those belonging to some sectarian faith will wrongly consider that *sanatana-dharma* is also sectarian, but if we go deeply into the matter and consider it in the light of modern science, it is possible for us to see that *sanatana-dharma* is the business of all the people of the world—nay, of all the living entities of the universe.

Non-*sanatana* religious faith may have some beginning in the annals of human history, but there is no beginning to the history of *sanatana-dharma*, because it remains eternally with the living entities. Insofar as the living entities are concerned, the authoritative *sastras* state that the living entity has neither birth nor death. In the *Gita* it is stated that the living entity is never born and he never dies. He is eternal and indestructible, and he continues to live after the destruction of his temporary material body. In reference to the concept of *sanatana-dharma*, we must try to understand the concept of religion from the Sanskrit root meaning of the word. *Dharma* refers to that which is constantly existing with a particular object. We conclude that there is heat and light along with the fire; without heat and light, there is no meaning to the word fire. Similarly, we must discover the essential part of the living being, that part which is his constant companion. That constant companion is his eternal quality, and that eternal quality is his eternal religion. (18-20)

Bhaktivedanta Swami Prabhupada wished to assure all who read his *Gita* translation that it was not a sectarian message, but the science of loving God. One might be a Hindu in this life, a Christian in the next, or a Muslim in the past, but in all cases one is a servant of God. To explain the details of that service is the purpose of religion, the rules and prohibitions the means, love of God the end.

A broad definition of religion as *sanatana-dharma* allows for truly universal religious belief based not on secondary natures but upon the primary nature of the soul proper. Stripped not only of our external social, cultural, and geographic dress, but also of the subtle underclothing of sectarian propositions, one stands revealed as a naked soul, a servant before the one God. In the transcendental abode of God, all have an intimate relationship with the Lord. With unalloyed love and devotion, the soul will worship God, and in so doing, rise above all sectarian designations.

CHAPTER 9

Religious Ethics:

The Relation of God to Morality

When I first informed my family members of my new-found faith in Krishna, I sent them a copy of the *Bhagavad-gita* to familiarize them with my new beliefs. One, a confirmed agnostic, after reading the *Gita* questioned, "How can you believe in a God who sanctions killing?" Still somewhat unfamiliar with my new religion's teachings and having been raised to admire pacifism, I was at a loss for a proper response. In retrospect I now understand that my relative chose to challenge my faith not by directly questioning the existence of God, but by questioning the basis of God's actions. If God's actions are immoral, what is the lesson for humanity? On a broader scale, what exactly is the relationship of ethics and religion, and, as my relative would have advocated, is a 'religionless' ethics really possible? After considering the main theories of the *acquisition* of moral knowledge, explaining how these theories handle the problem of the *diversity* of ethical principles, and evaluating the arguments of religionless ethicist Kai Nielsen, I shall offer my recently deceased relative a reply in memorial, based on nearly thirty years of assimilating Krishna's teachings.

Before discussing the acquisition of ethical truth, we need to know its source. Ethical principles are not simply *descriptive*, relating to what persons *actually* believe or how they *actually* behave. Rather, they essentially refer to what they *ought to* believe and how they *ought to* behave. Thus, they are *prescriptive* or *normative* principles.

What, then, is the source of such normative ethics? Is it God, or humans, or perhaps some other origin? Of course the vast majority of religious persons hold that at least in some respect, it is God. Some of these might argue that ethical principles are not directly God's commandments, yet are still connected with God. They might argue that, for example, it is wrong to inflict pain upon others unnecessarily. This ethical principle may not have been decreed by God, but it is obvious to anyone who can experience pain. Since God is responsible for creating beings who experience pleasure and pain, this particular 'truth' is *inherent* in his creation. It has, so to speak, always existed in God's mind (Peterson et al. 237).

But for many believers, such a theory of indirect origin does not go far enough. They prefer to see ethical principles as specific commandments that are a direct expression of God's will. A critic might question this assertion by asking whether this would obligate the believer to do anything God commands, even acts which we deem unethical.

Robert Adams responds by stating that we need not necessarily follow God's dictations because he is their origin, irrespective of what they may be. Rather, because we assume that God's character is, among other things, perfectly ethical, his commandments will always be just. By binding God's will to God's nature, the question of capricious dictums does not arise. "God, for instance, could not command us to kill innocent children 'just for the fun of it,' since this would be inconsistent with God's nature" (238). But, our critic might persist, could not God be a being who thought killing innocent children is actually a meritorious act? To which believers would respond that he might be, but the God we worship is not. Thus, it is perfectly reasonable to maintain that God is the source of the ethical principles we believe to be true.

We may now investigate how believers *acquire* ethical truths. There are three distinct possible responses most frequently given (241). The first is that ethical principles are communicated by God through some form of written revelation. Yet if this is so, why in every scripture do we find at least some statements that appear to be ethically questionable? Conservative believers respond to this doubt by acknowledging that God has the freedom to do as he likes. The principles under which he operates are not the same as those applicable to humans. This reply, of course, generates the next obvious question: How can such a double standard, one which may even violate our most basic moral conceptions, make God an endearing and admirable person? Most believers respond by stating that no such double standard actually exists; God "teaches by example."

Besides this "divine command" theory, there is also the "natural law" tradition of Thomas Aquinas (242). Humans made in God's image are capable of discovering the ethical standards revealed in nature. This is not to imply that human reason is a more trustworthy means of acquiring ethical truths than divine commandments. But reason can confirm these as well as discover many supplementary details.

Finally, a third possibility is that since humans are made in God's image, they possess the same *innate* ethical sense as God does. They are, in other words, the "ethical image" of God. They can understand intuitively, for example, that killing innocent children is wrong. Gottfried Leibniz points out that a certain degree of preliminary knowledge about what a child is and what killing is might be needed before we could reach our intuitive ethical conclusions. Along with this, additional information, written revelation, and reason might also be required. Still, some basic ethical principles are as inborn as traits, and need not be "learned" (243).

A serious problem arises with all of these three explanations. If believers acquire ethical principles by more or less the same means and from the same source (God), then why does there seem to be such a lack of ethical consensus among them? This diversity, believers respond, can be explained by the diversity in religious perspectives. They do not deny that written revelations may sometimes be incompatible. Granted that there would be such diverse opinions from differing religious traditions, why does there still seem to be so much diversity even *within* specific religions? Believers respond that a distinction must be drawn between "basic ethical principles and their practical application" (243). We can expect far more agreement on principles than in how they are to be applied. Diversity within a single religion can be further explained by differing factual assumptions. For example, although Jews and Christians would agree that taking an innocent life is wrong, they might disagree, in the case of a fetus, about what constitutes life. These answers allow believers to accommodate diversity without denying the sole source of their ethical beliefs.

It is observed, however, that often the diversity within a particular religious tradition is not merely in reference to practical applications or factual assumptions. Some differences are fundamental and relate to the *basic* principles themselves. For example, some Christians hold that it is never permissible to use life-threatening force, while others maintain that it may be justified to protect another innocent person's life. Given this fact, can believers still maintain that their religion has access to authoritative ethical truths? Believers often respond to this by explaining that the apparent differences are more issues of value judgments than differences in basic ethical principles. Peterson et al. cite an instance of Christians lying to the Nazis to protect Jews that they were hiding, while others did not (244). All the Christians were committed to protecting innocent lives *and* not lying. Therefore the differences arose in evaluating which principle was to be given priority.

Other believers explain that the differences are not differences in judgment as much as in human frailty. Specifically, they claim that ever since the "Fall," humans have lacked the capacity to fully understand ethical issues, and differences are due to their relative abilities to comprehend God's commandments. Finally, there is always the issue of cultural conditioning. Despite any innate sense of right and wrong, one rarely remains unaffected by one's environment.

The conclusion is that while one ought to acknowledge that ethical diversity exists even within individual religions, by no means does this invalidate the authoritative basis of their origin. The question must now be raised about non-believers. Can a non-religious person, or for that matter anyone who does not believe that ethical principles originate in God, have a basis for affirming ethical absolutes? Most non-believers would affirm that it is possible even though ethical truths originate in humankind. To understand their reasoning, it would be helpful to see how they respond to the believer's contention that God is an ultimate moral being. It may be recalled that God's commandments originate from God's will, which is ultimately tied to God's nature.

Religious critic Kai Nielsen questions the basis for believers' faith in God's goodness (239). There are only two possibilities, he insists. The first is that God's goodness is factual, or can be proven by evidential acts. But to this Nielsen argues that our judgment of God must be based on some prior standard of goodness. Hence, our own ethical intuitions are the ultimate standard, not God's commandments.

Nielsen posits the believer's second claim, namely that "goodness" is a necessary defining characteristic of "God." God's attitudes (or actions) would then be good simply because he possesses (or performs) them. Nielsen responds to this option, asking how believers know that the being from whom they supposedly have received these ethical principles is actually God. They cannot, he points out, claim that the being is God simply because the being is "good." Nor, conversely, can they claim that the actions of the being, or the being itself, is good simply because they believe the being is the all-powerful creator of the universe. Nielsen therefore concludes that the only way such believers can conclude that they are worshipping "God" is if they possess inherent and independent ethical standards of their own by which they can judge the being's actions and attitudes.

Having allowed Nielsen his due, Peterson et al. note that while believers may evaluate God by standards they had in mind before making their judgment, this does not necessarily mean that these standards existed separately from or were more fundamental than those of the being they judged (240). How can Nielsen be certain that it is not by God's influence that humans are capable of formulating such standards? After all, believers argue, God is the maker of humans and the environment in which they function; if humans judge God, it is only by a standard which God has given them the ability to construct. In this way believers stand up to Nielsen's arguments, holding fast to their claim that *ultimate* ethical authority resides solely in God.

Yet Nielsen insists that ethical standards can have an "'objective rationale in complete independence of religion'" (246). For example, "happiness is good" is not only an ethical principle that most persons know to be true; it is also normally most advantageous for all concerned. There is an obvious weakness in this argument, however. What if one's moral values were radically different from the norm? For example, what if one considers cheating or murder to be ethical? Nielsen's response is weak at best: he "'can only appeal to our sense of psychological realism to persuade us to admit intellectually what in practice we acknowledge. . . . to be moral involves respecting (human) rights'" (246). But these replies seem to beg the question.

What Nielsen really seems to be defining is more a type of "relative morality" than an "objective rationale." Unlike believers who would state that ethical principles exist *a priori* and are true for all persons at all times, Nielsen's morality is *a posteriori*, experientially based on rational considerations, to be affirmed at present. But considering the variance in human thought and the factor of changing circumstances, there seems little likelihood of any humanly conceived ethical absolutes. Still, Nielsen is not prepared to concede total relativism. While he acknowledges a certain degree of relativism, he still maintains that under normal conditions most persons will agree on what constitutes moral behavior.

Some have argued that Nielsen confuses factual with ethical issues—what *ought* to be affirmed should not be determined merely because certain acts *are* affirmed (247). Nielsen is quick to agree with the distinction, and turns the argument around to deny believers the right to insist that we ought to do whatever God commands because they think a being called God exists. However, he adds that factual claims do fortify moral claims.

Nielsen has made a strong point. A religious or a non-religious *ought* cannot be deduced from an *is*. And furthermore, both religious and non-religious persons strengthen their claims by appealing to factual contentions. Thus, there is some basis for a non-religiously based ethics. But since it rests on human beings who are variable, it can never be as absolute as a divinely inspired moral system. It need not degenerate to total relativity, however, for humans are rational, and, as Nielsen insists, under normal circumstances do seem to agree on certain principles of morality.

Having toured briefly the possibilities of religious and non-religious ethics, let us consider the subject from the monotheistic Vaishnava perspective of a Krishna devotee. We may recall the promise I made my deceased relative. While still alive, he inquired how I could worship a God who, in his estimation, sanctioned immorality.

The reader unfamiliar with the *Bhagavad-gita* will need a few details for my relative's question to make sense. Just prior to the outset of a great fratricidal war, Arjuna (a warrior by caste) argues with Krishna against fighting. His reasons are based on ethical principles: (a) his opponents include many relatives, elders, teachers, and dependents—all of whom deserve to be either respected or protected, but never killed; (b) with the destruction of his dynasty, family traditions will be vanquished and the rest of the family involved in irreligion; (c) without proper guidance and protection, the female family members will become degraded, and unwanted progeny will result; and (d) offerings to the ancestors, and all kinds of community projects and welfare activities will then cease. Arjuna concludes that it would be better to die in the battlefield unarmed and unresisting than incur the reactions of committing such sins. Having cast aside his weapons, his mind distraught, Arjuna appeals to Krishna for guidance.

Who can argue with Arjuna's reasons? They are based on reason, are full of compassion, and are supported by scriptural commands. Yet surprisingly, Lord Krishna criticizes Arjuna for being foolish, inconsiderate, and irreligious. To explain fully Krishna's reasoning would take us beyond our present purpose (Lord Krishna had to speak the entire philosophy of the *Gita* before Arjuna became convinced). But at least we can begin to unravel Lord Krishna's apparently paradoxical response. Krishna is speaking equivocally, referring to two sets of ethical standards. These two levels are described by A. C. Bhaktivedanta Swami Prabhupada:

> There are two kinds of *sva-dharmas*, specific duties. As long as one is not liberated, one has to perform the duties of his particular body in accordance with religious principles in order to achieve liberation. When one is liberated, one's *svadharma*—specific duty—becomes spiritual and is not in the material bodily concept. In the bodily conception of life there are specific duties for the *brahmanas* [teachers/priests] and *ksatriyas* [warriors/administrators] respectively, and such duties are unavoidable. *Sva-dharma* is ordained by the Lord, and this will be clarified in the Fourth Chapter. On the bodily plane *sva-dharma* is called *varnasrama-dharma*, or man's steppingstone for

spiritual understanding. Human civilization begins from the stage of *varnasrama-dharma*, or specific duties in terms of the specific modes of nature of the body obtained. Discharging one's specific duty in any field of action in accordance with the orders of higher authorities serves to elevate one to a higher status of life. (Purport, 2:31)

Arjuna's ethical reasons for discontinuing the war were certainly *sva-dharmic*, appropriate specific duties. Yet Lord Krishna wanted Arjuna to fight, and by doing so, to rise to the higher, liberated understanding of *sva-dharma*. His advice, though apparently inconsistent with worldly morality, helped Arjuna to transcend the duality of such worldly considerations. As Prabhupada explains in a later purport, "There is no consideration of happiness or distress, profit or gain, victory or defeat in the activities of Krishna consciousness. That everything should be performed for the sake of Krishna consciousness is transcendental consciousness; so there is no reaction [*karma*] to material activities" (2.38). This of course reminds us of the doubt raised when we first considered how believers acquire their ethical truths. Reasoning of this sort can easily be misused to promote either unethical principles or at least a double standard. Before we respond specifically to this valid concern, however, it would help to understand what is the source of ethical truth according to the Vaishnavas.

Clearly it is not of human origin. While conceding that there may be a general consensus of what falls within the broad categories of morality and immorality, the human condition is far too variable for the Vedic sages to base their judgment upon it. Time, place, circumstance, social position, etc.—all may determine one's ethical beliefs. The Vaishnavas therefore maintain that it is the eternally constant and omniscient Godhead alone who is capable of enunciating perfect truths. The proof text they cite in this regard is from the *Bhagavata Purana* (6.3.19), spoken by Yamaraja, the god who judges the dead:

Real religious principles are enacted by the Supreme Personality of Godhead. Although fully situated in the mode of goodness, even the great rsis [sages] who occupy the topmost planets cannot ascertain the real religious principles, nor can the demigods or the leaders of Siddhaloka [a planet of perfected souls], to say nothing of the asuras [intelligent demons], ordinary human beings, Vidyadharas and Caranas [celestial beings].

In his commentary to this verse, Bhaktivedanta Swami Prabhupada explains what "the real religious principles" are:

Herein it is stated that the real religious principle is that which is given by the Supreme Personality of Godhead. That principle is stated in *Bhagavad-gita. Sarva-dharman parityajya mam ekam saranam vraja*: one should give up all other duties and surrender unto the lotus feet of Krishna. That is the real religious principle everyone should follow. Even though one follows Vedic scriptures one may not know this transcendental principle, for it is not known to everyone. To say nothing of human beings, even demigods in the upper planetary systems are unaware of it. This transcendental religious principle must be understood from the Supreme Personality of Godhead directly or from His special representative.

As we can see, we are again dealing with two levels of ethical systems. The ultimate religious principle—surrender to God—may not necessarily be known to a follower of the Vedic scriptures, who may be of impeccable morality. But again, let us defer this discussion to first clarify how humans acquire their moral knowledge.

How exactly, according to Vaishnavas, does God deliver religious principles? Krishna explains his advent to Arjuna:

Whenever and wherever there is a decline in religious practice, O descendant of Bharata, and a predominant rise of irreligion—at that time I descend Myself. (4:7)

As we have seen from the earlier statement of Yamaraja, this is a "divine command" philosophy. God descends and speaks the *Bhagavad-gita*, meaning literally "the song of God." The Vedas are considered his "breathing." Sometimes he descends personally, and sometimes he sends his bona fide representative in the form of his son, or servant, or himself in some disguised form. In all cases he promotes the principles of religion as much as they can be understood by the particular people under their particular circumstances. But the ultimate intention is to induce full surrender.

God teaches by his words *and* actions. In another appropriate text of the *Gita*, Lord Krishna acknowledges his own responsibility for establishing proper conduct:

> If I did not perform prescribed duties, all these worlds would be put to ruination. I would be the cause of creating unwanted population, and I would thereby destroy the peace of all living beings. (3:24)

The Lord's general behavior is suitable for humans to follow. But at times it does happen that he oversteps morality, and believers must have the discriminatory power to know that they should not imitate him. In the important purport to the above text, Prabhupada allays the doubt of a double standard by distinguishing between *following* and *imitating*:

> We should, however, note carefully that although we have to follow in the footsteps of the Lord, we still have to remember that we cannot imitate Him. Following and imitating are not on the same level. We cannot imitate the Lord by lifting Govardhana Hill, as the Lord did in His childhood. It is impossible for any human being. We have to follow His instructions, but we may not imitate Him at any time. The *Srimad-Bhagavatam* (10.33.30-31) affirms: "One should simply follow the instructions of the Lord and His empowered servants. Their instructions are all good for us, and any intelligent person will perform them as instructed. However, one should guard against trying to imitate their actions. One should not try to drink the ocean of poison in imitation of Lord Siva."

We should always consider the movements of the *isvaras*, or those who can actually control the movements of the sun and moon, as superior. Without such power, one cannot imitate the *isvaras*, who are superpowerful. Lord Siva drank poison to the extent of swallowing an ocean, but if any common man tries to drink even a fragment of such poison, he will be killed. There are many pseudo devotees of Lord Siva who want to indulge in smoking *ganja* (marijuana) and similar intoxicating drugs, forgetting that by so imitating the acts of Lord Siva they are calling death very near. Similarly, there are some pseudo devotees of Lord Krishna who prefer to imitate the Lord in His *rasa-lila*, or dance of love, forgetting their inability to lift Govardhana Hill. It is best, therefore, that one not try to imitate the powerful, but simply follow their instruction; nor should one try to occupy their posts without qualification. There are so many "incarnations" of God without the power of the Supreme Godhead.

With this distinction in mind and with some sense of how the Vaishnavas view the human acquisition of moral truths, let us now turn to the intriguing issue of the two distinct categories of ethical instruction. We have already seen this principle at work in the discussion between Krishna and Arjuna at the outset of the war. Another vivid example is the famous Puranic narrative about the boy saint Prahlada. A half-lion half-man incarnation of God named Nrisimhadeva killed Prahlada's father while the boy stood nearby without protesting. What boy would stand by watching his father being killed? Certainly this appears highly immoral. To make matters seemingly worse, Prahlada prepared a garland of flowers and placed it upon the neck of his father's killer, expressing his satisfaction and pleasure. From a worldly point of view, Prahlada's behavior is reprehensible. Yet he is praised as one of the greatest saints in Vedic history. How are we to justify what appears to be a clear case of immorality?

We are dealing here with an issue similar to the Christians who lied to protect Jews from their Nazi persecutors. Even though his father attempted to kill him on numerous occasions, Prahlada never disrespected his father nor harbored any malice towards him. But when the boy was in the presence of the incarnation of Godhead, he had to prioritize his moral convictions. When it came to choosing between his father and God, he chose to be on the side of God. In other words, he violated mundane morality to achieve a higher, transcendental objective. In doing so he followed the Vedic prescription to treat all other rules and regulations as subservient to the basic principle of serving God.

There is an interesting modern anecdote that relates to this story. Some years ago a case came before the Supreme Court of the State of California involving the death of a father who, it was claimed, died of heartbreak upon learning that his child had become a member of the Hare Krishna movement. At one point in the trial the prosecuting attorney produced a painting depicting the Prahlada saga and read the Puranic narrative to the judge. The moral was clear: Hare Krishnas endorse immoral acts.[1] Incidents of this sort underscore the dangers of the two-level ethical system. There are injunctions in every religion which may demand the believer to cross the boundary of mundane morality. These injunctions can easily be misused to sanction acts which not only transgress mundane morality but are totally abominable in the eyes of both God and human kind (witness the crusades, jihads, pogroms, etc.). Yet without maintaining the transcendental level, religion can become a mere set of worldly rules and regulations without an ultimate spiritual goal. The only way to insure that transgressions of morality do not lead to irreligion is to bear in mind the distinction between "following" and "imitating." Any questionable decisions which might lead to irreligion should always be referred to learned and moral persons for their wise counsel.

Ethical knowledge guides social intercourse and is essential to progressive human life. The Vedic believer would find it difficult

---

[1] The judge eventually awarded the family of the deceased $32 million in damages, a decision which was appealed and finally settled out of court for an undisclosed amount.

to approve Nielsen's concept of a "religionless" ethic, even by referring such principles to the lower category of mundane morality. For even mundane principles have a transcendental origin and, ultimately, a transcendent goal. By gradual improvement of character, persons are expected to one day qualify for liberation. Not only do the Vedic thinkers deny human ability independent of godly inspiration, but they insist on tying ethical behavior to an ultimate transcendental goal. *In this sense*, there is really no possibility of a "religionless" ethic.

May the soul of my family member rest in peace. Amen.

Philosophy and Theological Doctrine:

Christianity and Vaishnavism in Parallel

Throughout the centuries there has been a close connection between philosophy and theology. Philosophy has often been used as a basis for religious formulations and for critiquing religious conceptions. But all of this changed substantially in the contemporary era when most philosophers considered it their duty to attack hallowed theological beliefs. Most recently, however, philosophers are showing renewed interest in substantiating theological doctrines from a philosophical viewpoint—analyzing their conceptual function and assessing their rational intelligibility. Their interest is not to prove these doctrines true, but to interpret them, especially in the context of how they apply to modern life.

Each of the contemporary philosophers whom we will review is a Christian and has selected the most traditional Christian view as the point from which to begin discussion. There is a great diversity of views, both old and new, which will not be presented due to the limited scope of this study. Our purpose is not to offer a broad survey, nor even a thorough analysis of the doctrines and their respective interpretations. Rather, by sampling the work of these leading Christian thinkers, we may gain an understanding of the new direction philosophers in the field of religious studies are now taking.

We will also examine these same doctrines, often thought to

be exclusively Christian, from the perspective of Indian Vaishnavism. This may not only demonstrate that the beliefs are common to religious traditions other than Christianity, but, due to the strong monotheistic nature of Vaishnavism, may provide the basis for further Christian insight. Our purpose will not be to engage in critical dialogue, but rather to expose Christian and Vaishnava concepts to modern sympathetic scrutiny.

The Incarnation

I believe in God the Father Almighty, maker of heaven and earth; and in Jesus Christ His only Son our Lord.

(Apostles' Creed)

Fools deride Me when I descend in the human form. They do not know My transcendental nature as the Supreme Lord of all that be.

(Bhagavad-gita 9:11)

The Christian doctrine of the incarnation presents Jesus Christ as simultaneously *fully human* and *fully divine* (255). Some modern believers have begun to question whether such a belief is actually rational. Thomas Morris is one philosopher who has defended this doctrine not to prove its truth-claim, but rather to demonstrate that its critics have failed to prove that it is irrational. The most common of the current criticisms is that the doctrine of incarnation is incoherent. This argument hinges on what the essential qualities of a human are in contrast to the essential qualities of a divine being. Humans are fallible and imperfect in so many ways, while God is the all-perfect, complete being. This appears to be an irresolvable contradiction.

Morris handles this issue by distinguishing between a thing being *fully* what it is and *merely* what it is. Jesus, like any of us, was *fully* human. But Jesus was much more. He shared the qualities of the Godhead; he was not a *mere* human. He was also *fully* God.

How will this line of reasoning explain Jesus's activities, for example, as an infant 'crying' and as a young boy 'struggling' to learn. This hardly resembles the all-knowing, all-perfect Being we are accustomed to think of. Morris resolves this apparent paradox with the theory of "two distinct ranges of consciousness" (256). Jesus, the God-Man, possessed an all-knowing divine consciousness, while at the same time possessing a thoroughly human consciousness which wrestled with events in a typically human manner. The two function simultaneously, the divine containing the human, but with the human aspect not having access to the divine. Thus, Jesus is not 'acting' when he experiences temptation, suffering, etc.

Another argument that Morris confronts is the popular claim that doctrines like the incarnation are not in sync with scientific advances. For example, it may have made perfect sense for persons living in biblical times to conceive of God's taking a human form. But this geocentric world-view is not relevant today, when humans are no longer the center of what we now know to be a vast, variegated universe. Morris dismisses this challenge, arguing that there is no reason to suggest that God cannot extend his interest to every detail of the universe (including humans); the fact that humans may not occupy the center stage is no reason to conclude that this means they are actually less important.

If Morris's defense holds, then exactly how does one maintain a rational belief in the incarnation? While Morris admits that there is no precise or single deductive argument to establish this fact, he suggests that there may be an innate human capacity which allows humans to recognize God under various circumstances (257). Christians may in fact be experiencing God Incarnate in any number of ways (prayer, for example), and there is no special reason to think that they are not. Without proof to the contrary, Morris contends that those believing in the incarnation have every rational right to continue.

The concept of incarnation appears frequently in Vaishnava theology. Unlike Christian doctrine which designates Jesus as the single incarnation of God, the ancient Sanskrit texts inform us that there are as many incarnations as there are waves in the ocean. Among these, ten are especially prominent, of whom Krishna and Rama are the most famous. But Krishna's position is different than all others: the incarnations are called *avataras* (literally "ones who descend"), whereas Krishna is referred to as the *avatari* (the source of all other *avataras*). Not only is there a distinction between the *avatari* and *avataras*, but amongst the *avataras* there are many categories. For example, some are empowered incarnations (*shaktyavesha avatara*). This refers to a type of 'power of attorney' by which an individual is empowered with a specific divine potency to fulfill a particular mission. Thus Vyasadeva, traditionally said to be the author of the Vedas, is empowered with the ability to compile the Vedas, while sage Narada is empowered with the potency to induce devotion for God. These empowered incarnations do not have all the potencies of the Godhead, but only one or two, and then only as much of these potencies as is required to fulfill their mission. Krishna, however, is the Godhead, complete with all potencies to the maximum degree. According to the Vaishnavas, this makes him unique.

The "two distinct ranges of consciousness" referred to by Morris is a concept commonly employed by Vaishnavas to explain the incarnation. In some ways it is more applicable to the empowered incarnations, for their bodies are truly human as was Jesus's. Krishna's was "human-like," for he is said to have descended to Earth with his self-same body as he displays in the kingdom of God.

Despite this difference, the explanation in regard to Krishna's incarnation is still relevant to our discussion. For Krishna, being God, has the capacity to make his body develop much as that of an ordinary human. This phenomenon is described by A. C. Bhaktivedanta Swami Prabhupada in a purport to his *Bhagavad-gita As It Is* (4:6):

Krishna appears in this material world in His original eternal form, with two hands, holding a flute. He appears exactly in His eternal body, uncontaminated by this material world. Although He appears in this same transcendental body and is Lord of the universe, it still appears that He takes His birth like an ordinary living entity. And although His body does not deteriorate like a material body, it still appears that Lord Krishna grows from childhood to boyhood and from boyhood to youth. But astonishingly enough He never ages beyond youth. At the time of the Battle of Kuruksetra, He had many grandchildren at home; or, in other words, He had sufficiently aged by material calculations. Still He looked just like a young man twenty or twenty-five years old. We never see a picture of Krsna in old age because He never grows old like us, although He is the oldest person in the whole creation—past, present, and future. Neither His body nor His intelligence ever deteriorates or changes. Therefore, it is clear that in spite of His being in the material world, He is the same unborn, eternal form of bliss and knowledge, changeless in His transcendental body and intelligence.

Many of the activities Krishna displayed in this world are recorded in the *Bhagavata Purana's* Tenth Canto. While playing with his mother, for instance, he exhibits all of the symptoms of an ordinary child: he 'cries' to drink her breast milk, 'laughs' when she tickles him, is 'thoughtful' when admonished, and 'fears' her reprimands. It is these very human-like qualities, not his almighty Godliness, that make Krishna so attractive and have won him such wide-spread and avid a following. His humanness is so deceiving that great personalities like Brahma (the first created being who later 'creates,' or more correctly 'engineers' the universe) become bewildered upon seeing Krishna's activities. Even Krishna himself becomes mystified by his human pastimes and forgets his Godship.

The *Bhagavata* commentators wrestle with the same issue that Morris confronts: How can the all-powerful Godhead be so humanly compromised? The resolution to this apparent dilemma, they inform us, can be understood with reference to the godly potency known as *yogamaya*. *Maya* or *shakti* is the energy of

God. God possesses innumerable such *shaktis*, each of whom fulfills a particular need. The *yogamaya-shakti* is one such energy. *Yoga* means "union" and *maya* means "illusion." Vedic injunctions enjoin that we come out of *maya's* grip, out of illusion. But *yogamaya* is different than the illusionary *maya* whose grip we must escape. *Yogamaya* is favorable because she helps unite us with the Deity.

While ordinary *Maya* has jurisdiction over conditioned souls, *Yogamaya's* jurisdiction extends to liberated souls. More significantly in terms of our immediate topic, the Godhead himself agrees to come under her influence. *Yogamaya* casts her spell upon God and his devotees in such a manner that he forgets that he is infinite while they forget that they are finite. Thus she closes the gap between God and the devotees. With this imagined equality they are able to experience human-like exchanges which would be ordinarily impossible if either God or the devotees were to remember the many differences which ordinarily separate them. Devotees thus relate to God in friendship, parental affection, or conjugal love, and the Lord reciprocates accordingly.

But is God's incarnation only for those of this earth, and more specifically, especially for humans? The Vaishnava response to this "'geocentric challenge'" (Peterson et al. 257) is that God incarnates not only amongst humans on this planet, but amongst a vast variety of species and in many places throughout the universe. Here, for example, is a verse from the *Bhagavata Purana*, recited by the principal demigods as they stood unseen, offering prayers to Krishna as he lay within the womb of his mother:

> O Supreme controller, Your Lordship previously accepted incarnations as a fish, a horse, a tortoise, Narasimhadeva [a lion], a boar, a swan, Lord Ramacandra, Parasurama and, among the demigods, Vamanadeva, to protect the entire world by Your mercy. Now please protect us again by Your mercy by diminishing the disturbances in this world. O Krishna, best of the Yadus, we respectfully offer our obeisances unto You. (10.2.40)

Nor does this limit Krishna's care to Earth alone. The incarnation of Vamana is said to have benefited inhabitants in all the planetary systems (Vedic cosmography does not restrict life only to the planet Earth). Another incarnation, Lord Paramatma or the Supersoul, is said to be present as the indwelling witness within all of creation. Krishna speaks of this when he tells Arjuna in the *Gita*: "With a single fragment of Myself I pervade and support this entire universe" (10:42). Krishna is within everything and simultaneously everything is within Krishna. Brahma, the first-born, explains this doctrine as follows:

> He is an undifferentiated entity as there is no distinction between potency and the possessor thereof. In His work of creating millions of universes, His potency remains inseparable. All of the universes exist in Him and He is present in His fullness in every one of the atoms that are scattered throughout the universe at one and the same time. Such is the primeval Lord whom I adore. (*Sri Brahma-samhita* 5.35)

If, through the agency of the Supersoul, all the worlds exist in Krishna and Krishna resides simultaneously in fullness and entirety in all the atoms in all the worlds, the "geocentric challenge" is easily dismissed.

The Vaishnavas try to present rational support for the belief in the incarnation. As to *how* it is possible for a rational person to hold such a belief, the Vaishnavas suggest, much as Morris does, that there is "innate human capacity" which makes it possible. This specific quality is known as *bhakti*, or "loving devotion." It is the intrinsic nature of the soul, once freed of all material conditioning, to love God. This is explained by Bhaktivedanta Swami Prabhupada in the *Nectar of Instruction*:

> The understanding of Krishna consciousness is innate in every living entity, and it is already developed to some extent when the living entity takes a human body. It is said in *Chaitanya-charitamrita* (*Madhya* 22.107): "Pure love for Krsna is eternally established in the

hearts of living entities. It is not something to be gained from another source. When the heart is purified by hearing and chanting, the living entity naturally awakens." Since Krsna consciousness is inherent in every living entity, everyone should be given a chance to hear about Krsna. Simply by hearing and chanting—*sravanam kirtanam*—one's heart is directly purified, and one's original Krsna consciousness is immediately awakened. Krsna consciousness is not artificially imposed upon the heart, it is already there. When one chants the holy name of the Supreme Personality of Godhead, the heart is cleansed of all mundane contamination. (41)

Thus, whether by chanting God incarnate's holy names, hearing of his activities, seeing his portrait or other worshipable image, or through prayer, a devotee experiences the reality of the incarnation. And just as Morris concludes, there is no reason to believe that this is not actually the case and perfectly reasonable to think that it is so.

The Atonement

Having become the sin of all men, he washed away the sin of the human race.
(St. Ambrose)

Abandon all varieties of religion and just surrender unto Me. I shall deliver you from all sinful reactions. Do not fear.
(Bhagavad-gita 18:66)

Traditional Christian belief held that humans had fallen from God's grace ever since Adam and Eve's original sin, but that this relationship with God could be reestablished due to the suffering and death of Jesus Christ. Contemporary thinkers have been reassessing this doctrine, trying to more precisely understand Christ's redeeming role. Philip Quinn has been especially interested in evaluating Thomas Aquinas's position on these matters (Peterson et al. 258).

Aquinas believed that sin affects humans in three ways. First, it stains our souls, causing us to act in ways contrary to reason and divine law. Second, the devil as a powerful influence exists independently of our tendency to misbehave. Lastly, our grievous sinfulness is deserving of eternal damnation. Aquinas admits that God could have exonerated us from such punishment, but his severity in not always doing so does not make him unjust.

The problem, as Aquinas saw it, was that the compounded sinfulness committed by Adam and humankind against the infinite Godhead was infinite in magnitude with no possibility of proper repayment. The only solution was for God to settle the terms of restitution by personally paying through Christ's suffering and death. In fact, Christ's own divinity, the quality and quantity of his love, and the magnitude of his suffering was far greater recompense than God's justice required.

Quinn responds with the most obvious questions (259). What need is there for anyone else to suffer? If Christ has paid sufficiently, why do we still see individuals suffer in this life and hear that they may suffer in a future hell? Aquinas offers the answer that humans must appropriate or claim Christ's payment through such sacraments as baptism, penance, etc., or else they will not be freed from their debt.

While Quinn finds this response acceptable, he is not satisfied with Aquinas's depiction of the devil's role. Is the devil merely an agent of God justly awarding punishment? Or is he an unjust overlord demanding that we pay him what was rightly due to God? Quinn wishes that Aquinas had selected one explanation or the other. His own proposal is that we give up the idea that Christ's atonement ransomed sinners from Satan and think instead that it simply redeemed us in the eyes of God.

Quinn is also troubled by Aquinas's apparently harsh theory that without baptism there is no possibility of redemption. This automatically bars unbaptized infants and those who may have never heard of God from ever entering heaven. Quinn prefers that the terms of Christ's atonement be changed: unfortunates of either category should be guaranteed salvation through Christ's atonement.

But the viewpoint of Aquinas that Quinn finds most disturbing is the belief that *Christ's* death constitutes an acceptable payment for *our* debt. Perhaps, Quinn reasons, such a monetary nomenclature was appropriate to times past when pardons for crimes as severe as murder could be legally bought by monetary payments. But our present morality (and legal structure as well) is significantly different, and one can no longer *pay* for another's crimes, let alone be punished as a proxy. To transfer just punishment to a totally innocent person is, therefore, unacceptable.

Quinn presents his solution in the form of a fable (260). In the story, a wealthy man appoints two of his sons as stewards of his estate. The elder son fails miserably to maintain the father's holdings, while the younger succeeds admirably. Though the elder deserves to be punished for his neglect, the younger agrees voluntarily to assume responsibility for the entire property as an act of service to his older brother. As a result of the younger son's outstanding service, the father, rather than disinheriting the elder son, is moved to show him mercy.

Quinn's fable still includes an element of repayment, but lays stress on the act of generating mercy. It indicates that Christ sacrificed himself for us not to pay our debt so much as to generate divine mercy. Thus, the orthodox requirement of Christ as the necessary via media for human reconciliation with God is maintained, while the explanation for the act no longer disturbs our moral reason.

The atonement may appear to be a specifically Christian concept, depending, as it seems to, on Christ's sacrifice. Yet as we have indicated earlier, as the Vedic/Vaishnavite tradition gives no less importance to the incarnation, we may expect that it will also address the issue of atonement. For why else does Godhead incarnate if not for redeeming the sinful?

A fundamental difference occurs at the outset. Sinfulness, according to the Vedas, is not the fault of some original ancestor. The guilt is placed squarely upon each individual soul. It is *we* who have chosen to turn away from God. If anything, this only increases the burden of each individual's guilt, for there is no Adam to share the blame. Yet the image of God is not nearly so severe as the Christian portrayal. There is no final judgment, nor any eternal hell. Instead, the sinful are given innumerable opportunities (through reincarnation) to liquidate their "debt."

But our reformative efforts are constantly foiled by a powerful agent: *Maya*. This is not the *Maya* whom we met previously. *Yogamaya*, as we may recall, was favorable to our relationship with God; this *Maya*, on the other hand, is the external manifestation of *Yogamaya*, meant to keep us in bondage. *Maya's* action is two-fold: *prakshepatmika-shakti*, the spell of diversion, which impels one to remain in conditioned life fully satisfied by sense enjoyment; and *avaranatmika-shakti*, by which a soul feels pleasure in even the most degraded condition. *Maya's* illusionary spell in many ways resembles the work of Satan. And, as some Christian theologians have portrayed Satan as God's assistant, *Maya* is understood as God's maidservant:

> The external potency Maya who is of the nature of the shadow of the *cit* potency, is worshipped by all people as Durga, the creating, preserving and destroying agency of this mundane world. I adore the primeval Lord Govinda [another name for Krishna] in accordance with whose will Durga conducts herself. (*Sri Brahma-samhita* 5.44)

Entrusted with the thankless task of keeping the sinful imprisoned within material existence, *Maya* feels ashamed to stand directly before the Lord.

The conditioned souls, transmigrating through innumerable births, are pushed forward by their own desires while being simultaneously allured by *Maya's* enticements. From time to time they make efforts to atone for their sins, for they are warned by scripture that failure to do so will lead to more suffering both in this lifetime and the next. Yet despite such efforts to improve, souls continue to sin. This stark reality was observed by a pious king named Pariksit:

> Sometimes one who is very alert so as not to commit sinful acts is victimized by sinful life again. I therefore consider this process of repeated sinning and atoning to be useless. It is like the bathing of an elephant, for an elephant cleanses itself by taking a full bath, but then throws dust over its head and body as soon as it returns to the land. (*Bhagavata Purana* 6.1.10)

The type of atonement mentioned here falls under the category of *punya*, "pious activities," as distinguished from *bhakti*, loving devotional service. Piousness cancels sinfulness—act for act—but does not uproot the cause of sinfulness. This can only be accomplished, as the pious king is told, by the performance of devotional service to God. Which brings us to the *Gita* verse cited at the outset.

In that verse (18:66), Lord Krishna recommends that one should "abandon all varieties of religion." By this he means all varieties of piety. For, as the king understood, atonement through pious acts is not permanently purifying any more than is an elephant's bathing. Krishna therefore recommends surrender, and it is specifically to facilitate and accept the surrender of his devotees that he incarnates with the purpose of facilitating and accepting the surrender of his devotees. He promises protection from all sinful reactions to whomsoever surrenders to him.

But in what way does Krishna sacrifice on behalf of the sinful? Is there any indication that he has suffered as Christ did? For, as we have already noted, it is the magnitude of Christ's suffering that is of utmost importance to the issue of atonement. But is the act of suffering and death an absolutely necessary condition for human reconciliation with God? Has God only a wrathful visage, and will he be appeased only by such a "blood libel"? If he is actually independent, and since it is he who was actually wronged, God can (as Aquinas admits) pardon us without exacting a penalty. That he did not do so in the case of Jesus is *not* at issue. But that Jesus was his sole atoning agent *is*.

Religions other than Christianity also make redemptive claims. Krishna does so in the above-cited *Gita* verse. So too, do other incarnations. There is even the extraordinary incidence of Vasudeva Datta, a sixteenth-century Vaishnava saint who prayed as follows:

> My dear Lord, You incarnate just to deliver all conditioned souls. I have now one petition, which I wish You would accept. My Lord, You are certainly capable of doing whatever You like, and You are indeed merciful. If You so desire, You can easily do whatever You want. My Lord, my heart breaks to see the sufferings of all conditioned souls; therefore I request You to transfer the karma of their sinful lives upon my head. My dear Lord, let me suffer perpetually in a hellish condition, accepting all the sinful reactions of all living entities. Please finish their diseased material life. (*Sri Chaitanya-caritamrita, Madhya-lila* 15.160-163)

Let us consider the extent of Vasudeva's offering. While Jesus and Krishna both offered deliverance to their followers (and even, it may be argued, to many others as well), the devotee Vasudeva was prepared to accept the sinful reactions of "all conditioned souls." The method of atonement he proposed was to suffer perpetually in hell. Certainly these are traditional conditions of atonement.

Of course one may wonder if Vasudeva's prayers were effective. Vasudeva made his proposal to Sri Chaitanya, an incarnation of Krishna, who responded in the following manner:

> Whatever a pure devotee wants from his master, Lord Krsna doubtlessly grants because He has no duty other than to fulfill the desire of His devotee. If you desire the deliverance of all living entities within the universe, then all of them can be delivered even without

your undergoing the tribulations of sinful activity. Krsna is not incapable, for He has all potencies. Why would He induce you to suffer the sinful reactions of other living entities? Whosoever welfare you desire immediately becomes a Vaishnava, and Krsna delivers all Vaishnavas from the reactions of their past sinful activities. (*Sri Chaitanya-charitamrita, Madhya-lila* 15.166-169)

What seems to be important here is not the actual act of suffering, but the willingness to undergo such suffering. And, as with Quinn's fable, the real issue is not simply the payment of debt, but the generation of divine mercy. Judgment is, after all, up to God's discretion; if we grant God independence and full cognizance, then he must also be allowed the wisdom to judge Vasudeva's sincerity. There is nothing that prevents petitionary prayer from being as meaningful as an actual act of sacrifice. For suffering of the mind can be even more harsh than the suffering of the physical body; Vasudeva may have mentally consumed all the sins of the universe by the power of his compassion.

The Indwelling of the Holy Spirit

I believe in the Holy Ghost, the Lord, and Giver of Life, who proceedeth from the Father and Son.

(*Niceno-Chalcedonian Creed*)

Sri Krsna, the Personality of Godhead, who is the Paramatma [Supersoul] in everyone's heart and the benefactor of the truthful devotee, cleanses desire for material enjoyment from the heart of the devotee who has developed the urge to hear His messages, which are in themselves virtuous when properly heard and chanted.

(*Bhagavata Purana 1.2.17*)

Christian tradition terms our reconciliation with God through the intercession of Christ as *salvation*. *Sanctification*, on the other hand, is the on-going process of personal transformation, traditionally thought to be accomplished through the third person of the Trinity: the Holy Spirit. William Alston, dismissing as unorthodox the notion that the Spirit is uninvolved with such transformation, has attempted to evaluate the degree of responsibility assigned to God and, in addition, to human effort (Peterson et al. 262).

Alston considers three possibilities. The first, called the *Fiat* model, attributes our renewal wholly to God's doing, an act of grace much as salvation is. Although Alston acknowledges that God could in fact make things happen this way, he considers that God's creation is prescribed by individuality. This individuality appears to be particularly lacking in the *Fiat* model. Moreover, if divine will is all that is at work, why does the renewal process often seem to take so long? Alston therefore concludes that human effort must also be a significant factor.

A second perspective is the *interpersonal* model, by which God transforms us in much the same manner as we transform each other. Here the key term is *voluntary.* God calls us, chastises, encourages, energizes—but the choice to accept or reject his help is ours. Though Alston appreciates the element of personal involvement, he finds both this option and the one by *Fiat* lacking in that both situate God as an agent working from without. Traditional Christian doctrine explains that the Holy Spirit *dwells within* us. The Bible states that we should be "*filled, permeated, pervaded* with the Spirit" (263).

Alston therefore prefers a third model, that of *sharing.* In this understanding, the Spirit dwells within us, and we partake of its divine nature. Alston clarifies that he is not speaking of the individual's becoming one with God. We still retain our individuality with the capacity to sin; but the lines of demarcation between the divine and ourselves are no longer so rigid. Much as two humans living in close proximity would exert manifold influences upon each other, our intimacy with the Holy Spirit enables us to share in its nature and thus become transformed. Alston wants to insure that the sharing is voluntary;

though we know what is God's desire and feel inclined to fulfill it, the final act is a demonstration of our free will.

Is there a Vaishnava parallel to the doctrine of the Indwelling Spirit? The verse selected from the *Bhagavata Purana* at the outset of our present discussion would certainly suggest there is. The Vaishnavas conceive of the Paramatma or Supersoul as an expansion of the Godhead, situated within the heart of every living entity. In the *Bhagavad-gita* Lord Krishna identifies himself with that Supersoul:

> I am seated in everyone's heart, and from Me come remembrance, knowledge and forgetfulness. (15:15)

> The Supreme Lord is situated in everyone's heart, O Arjuna, and is directing the wanderings of all living entities . . . (18:61)

The presence of the Supersoul within all living beings is not dependent upon one's faith or any other consideration of worthiness. Rather, it is a sign of God's concern for all living entities, whom he loves as a father loves his children. As a caring father might not allow his errant children to be neglected, but might continue to monitor their movements and to benefit them even without their knowledge, so God takes up his residence within the heart and accompanies the wayward soul throughout its transmigrations.

It would seem that these verses of the *Gita* indicate a God who is fully in charge. God "is directing the wanderings of all living entities" and causes "remembrance, knowledge and forgetfulness." Is this the *Fiat* model which Alston rejected? Absolutely not; for God operates on the principle of 'man proposes, God disposes.' He does not use force, but reciprocates according to each individual's desires and efforts.

But this could leave God open to the criticism of indulging his children whimsically. After all, if he is prepared to fulfill whatever they desire, could he not be blamed for their degradation? A child may have its wishes, but not the means to satisfy them. It is only with the help of its parents that the child realizes the fulfillment of his wishes. Perhaps God has acted like a doting father and spoiled us?

This charge is unfair, the Vaishnavas would say. It may sometimes appear that a parent may find no better means to instruct a child than through some temporary suffering. A parent, for example, may warn a child of the dangers of fire. But seeing that the child disregards all warnings, the parent may quickly pass the child's hand over a candle flame for the purpose of teaching a lesson. It is not the parent's intention to inflict pain; quite the opposite. So the presence of the Supersoul within the heart is a sign of God's ultimate concern that his children not be misled. He offers them constant good counsel in the form of scripture, saintly association, and the voice of the inner conscience. However, he never overrides the free will he has gifted.

Thus, the *Fiat* model is inappropriate to the Vaishnava conception. The *interpersonal* model more approximates the idea, except, as Alston emphasizes, it places God "outside." Therefore it is the *sharing* model which most closely describes the Vaishnava conception. Alston's example of two humans whose lives are intimately entwined is expressed in the Upanishadic story of two birds sharing the same tree. A.C. Bhaktivedanta Swami Prabhupada illuminates this example:

> The Vedas, like the *Mundaka Upanisad*, as well as the *Svetasvatara Upanisad*, compare the soul and the Supersoul to two friendly birds sitting on the same tree. One of the birds (the individual atomic soul) is eating the fruit of the tree, and the other bird (Krsna) is simply watching His friend. Of these two birds—although they are the same in quality—one is captivated by the fruits of the material tree, while the other is simply witnessing the activities of His friend. Krsna is the witnessing bird, and Arjuna is the eating bird. Although they are friends, one is still the master and the other is the servant. Forgetfulness of this relationship by the atomic soul is the cause of

one's changing his position from one tree to another, or from one body to another. The *jiva* soul is struggling very hard on the tree of the material body, but as soon as he agrees to accept the other bird as the spiritual master—as Arjuna agreed to do by voluntary surrender unto Krsna for instruction—the subordinate bird immediately becomes free from all lamentations. Both the *Mundaka Upanisad* (3.1.2) and *Svetasvatara Upanisad* (4.7) confirm this: 'Although the two birds are in the same tree, the eating bird is fully engrossed with anxiety and moroseness as the enjoyer of the fruits of the tree. But if in some way or other he turns his face to his friend who is the Lord and knows His glories—at once the suffering bird becomes free from all anxieties.' (Purport, *Gita* 2:22)

The Supersoul wishes that the individual soul "becomes free from all anxieties." This is his real intention in agreeing to accompany the individual soul throughout its wanderings. As Krishna explains to Arjuna: "To show them special mercy, I, dwelling in their hearts, destroy with the shining lamp of knowledge the darkness born of ignorance" (10:11). When the individual soul becomes aware of the Supersoul's glories, the individual is, as Christians would say, "*saved.*" But the ongoing process of personal transformation, which they call *sanctification,* is accomplished through association with the Supersoul within, and by the association of saintly persons without.

Petitionary Prayer

The effectual fervent prayer of a righteous man availeth much.
(Holy Bible—K. J. V.)

My dear Lord, one who earnestly waits for You to bestow Your causeless mercy upon him, all the while patiently suffering the reactions for his past misdeeds and offering You respectful obeisances with his heart, words and body, is surely elligible for liberation, for it has become his rightful claim.
(Bhagavata Purana 10.14.8)

Believers of all religions often petition God for what they believe may not come about without divine assistance. This may be due to some perceived need that they hope that God will meet. But one may wonder what need there is to make such requests if God is indeed all-knowing and all-merciful? Will he not of his own accord send what we need when we need it? Elenore Stump, a modern philosopher of religion, examines Thomas Aquinas's answers to these questions.

Aquinas reasoned that our petitionary prayers are not meant to change God's will, but to indicate our readiness to receive what has already been allotted to us. Stump is not entirely satisfied with this response. She grants that God wants humans to pray and also that God fulfills such prayers, "'but why,'" she asks, "'should prayers be included in God's plan as causes of certain effects?'" (265)

Stump proposes a model that focuses upon God's loving relationship with us. The Bible often compares this God-human relationship to that of husband and wife, parent and child, or to that of two friends. But how is friendship possible with one as great as God? For friendship is seen to grow strongest the more the parties are equal. In the relationship with God, God looms above and beyond any possibility of equality. The human response to this is often one of sheer dependence.

Stump believes that God wants to forge a meaningful relationship with us. And to do so he allows an element of suspense to exist, in which we are not certain whether God will or will not respond to our needs. Unless we pray, he may not; and even if we do, he still may not. This makes the relationship very real, far more so than if God were automatically to fulfill our prayers.

Nor does God need to wait for our petitions to interfere with earthly affairs. He may do so at any time as he so wishes. Yet our prayers *can* influence him to become involved in a different manner. Stump's model allows God the ultimate control, while still offering a meaningful role to humans. And God is always free to act independently: he can fulfill our needs without being asked, and ignore them even when requested.

But what if petitions are offered on behalf of a third party? Would God not be meddling, invading another's privacy without invitation? Stump judges that God will only involve himself when asked by one person to help another when the third party "'has willingly shared his thoughts and feelings and the like with God'" (267). This may not be an entirely satisfying answer. It is even more difficult for Stump to resolve the problem of petitionary prayers that appeal for God's intervention in natural disasters. But Stump believes that her thoughts are in the right direction in reconciling the Christian need to see God as a loving, caring parent and the Christian belief that asking makes a difference.

Vaishnavas hold prayer to be of utmost importance within the overall process of devotional service to God. Through prayer, the devotee calls out to God, seeking recognition of a particular sort. The petitioner may be materially motivated or else spiritually inspired, but in either case addresses the appeal to the Godhead. For example, in the *Gita* Krishna acknowledges four types of petitioners:

> O best among the Bharatas, four kinds of pious men begin to render devotional service unto Me—the distressed, the desirer of wealth, the inquisitive, and he who is searching for knowledge of the Absolute.

Krishna goes on to explain to Arjuna that of these four, the first two are more materially inclined, while the last—the seeker of knowledge of the Absolute—is generally more sincere. But there are still other divisions, those who have transcended all material motivations as well as the realms of speculation, and who approach God out of pure love. Krishna judges these to be best.

Irrespective of one's motivations, what exactly is the role of prayer? And, according to the Vaishnavas, what demands do such petitions place upon God? Perhaps these questions can best be answered by examining various petitions and God's response to them.

An instance of a prayer offered for the attainment of wealth is found in the *Bhagavata Purana* narration of the young prince Dhruva. He approaches God to achieve a kingdom more exalted than any others. But in the course of having his prayer fulfilled, he comes to recognize the chimera of material things. As he puts it:

> Alas, just look at me! I am so unfortunate. I approached the lotus feet of the Supreme Personality of Godhead, who can immediately cut the chain of the repetition of birth and death, but still, out of foolishness, I prayed for things which are perishable. (4.9.31)

Here, God uproots a devotee's material desires. Indeed, we are informed further on in the text that while God may satisfy someone's material motives, he will not cause that person to demand more benedictions again. Rather, he will ultimately grant his own association, even though one may not aspire for it. Such an instance would be an example of God's exercising totally independent will in contravenance of an individual's expressed wish.

Yet there are numerous instances in which God withholds himself from his devotee, to increase the devotee's yearning. Thus the sage Narada was made to wait an entire lifetime, praying all the while, before having his desire to meet the Lord fulfilled. In fact, this is the case with most believers. They will pray throughout their lives, confident that God hears their prayers and will one day fulfill them. In this sense, the prayers themselves have an intrinsic power of satisfaction; though they may not immediately yield the desired results, the petitioner feels already connected with the Deity through the prayer. Thus, the reciprocation between God and the petitioner cannot be measured merely by externals.

The quality of the prayer may also be important in

determining the degree of reciprocation. God is not obliged to respond merely because he is addressed. A thief may pray to God for protection, but must God grant such a boon? If he does, will it not make God also a party to the crime? The *sincerity* and the *content* are to be considered.

For example, in a time of war family members pray to God for protection of their loved ones. Yet in spite of such prayers, many will not return home. Does it mean that God has not heard their prayers? Or were the individuals who prayed insincere? Perhaps more can be understood by the family's response on learning of their member's death. If they lose faith in God, perhaps they were not truly sincere. And God may very well have known this from the start. On the other hand, we cannot conclude that the family members of sincere believers will not be killed in battle. The contrary is too often the case. But the believing families' responses are telling: they will not lose their faith in God, but rather will accept that God knew what was best for their beloved relatives and arranged accordingly.

This issue of sincerity is addressed by Queen Kunti, the mother of Arjuna. In a remarkable series of prayers, she requests Krishna to send endless calamities upon her family, for this will force them to constantly take shelter of the Lord. Then she describes the qualifications for sincere prayer:

> My Lord, Your Lordship can easily be approached, but only by those who are materially exhausted. One who is on the path of material progress, trying to improve himself with respectable parentage, great opulence, high education and bodily beauty, cannot approach You with sincere feeling. (*Bhagavata Purana* 1.8.26)

If we accept that God is capable of personal relationships, can we not assume that he will distinguish the sincerity of those who approach him? Krishna assures Arjuna, "As all surrender unto Me, I reward them accordingly" (*Bhagavad Gita* 4:11). If, as Stump argues, God wishes to have a meaningful relationship with us, it would seem that he will certainly take note of our sincerity if sincerity be a necessary criterion for a meaningful relationship. And since it is necessary in human affairs, we have no reason to think it would not be so with God.

The preeminent Vaishnava authority Rupa Goswami categorizes levels of sincerity in terms of degrees of submission: 1) *samprar-thanatmika*, offering prayers with great feeling; 2) *dainyavodhika*, humbly submitting oneself; 3) *lalasamayi*, desiring some perfectional stage. But the ultimate in surrender was indicated by Lord Chaitanya, the most recent incarnation of Krishna, who happened also to be the spiritual master of Rupa Goswami. Lord Chaitanya prayed:

> I know no one but Krsna as my Lord, and He shall remain so even if He handles me roughly by His embrace or makes me brokenhearted by not being present before me. He is completely free to do anything and everything, for He is always my worshipful Lord unconditionally. (*Shikshashtakam* 8)

This is the example of total surrender, wherein God is given free license by the petitioner to respond in any manner he so desires. The petitioner (in this case Lord Chaitanya himself) is so deeply absorbed in loving relationship with God, that no external reciprocation is needed to satisfy the petition. Rather, the prayer is an expression of pure love which is seemingly without any demands, but which in fact makes the highest demand of all. God becomes bound by the depth of the devotee's love and willingly allows himself to become the possession of his devotee. This is the perfection of petitionary prayer.

In regard to petitions offered on behalf of a third party, the Vaishnavas assert that such prayers have great efficacy. They would disagree with Stump's conclusion that God's involvement in a third party's fortune without their prior 'consent' constitutes an invasion of privacy. To carry out an analogy Stump previously used, if God is a loving parent, it would not be wrong for him to grant a benediction to one of his children without their prior consent and involvement. It is natural for a parent to always want to see the children benefited, and the very nature of the parental relationship assumes (at least traditionally) that a parent has such a 'right.' This might not be so if the child was of a *mature* age. But if we consider the child in question to be spiritually *immature*, then the parent not only has the right but the obligation to interfere on the child's behalf.

Revelation

It is expedient to have . . . what God has revealed, in addition to the philosophical researches pursued by human reasoning.

(Thomas Aquinas)

Only unto those great souls who have implicit faith in both the Lord and the spiritual master are all the imports of Vedic knowledge automatically revealed.

(Svetashvatara Upanishad 6.23)

Our attempt thus far in this chapter, as well as in those before, has been to see the connections between reason and religious belief. But it is often thought that there are at least some aspects of how we come to know about God that can be understood only if they are *revealed* to us by God apart from any rational considerations. Does revelation actually take place, and if so, in exactly what manner? George Mavrodes has attempted to tackle these questions (Peterson et al. 268).

Mavrodes begins by defining revealed theology as those religious truths which lie beyond the range of reason. He extrapolates three models of revelation based upon this definition. The first he labels the *Causation Model*, which refers to what we normally call *innate knowledge*: religious truths which could not arise from our ordinary experiences in the ordinary world. This sort of innate knowledge can be understood in two ways. We encounter it in Plato's Socratic discussion in the *Meno*, where after questioning by Socrates, a slave boy exhibits a surprisingly sophisticated degree of knowledge. Plato explains that the boy was "born" with this knowledge, and it was stored in his memory until it was revived by Socrates's questions. Mavrodes also reminds us that Descartes believed that religious information, such as the belief in God, is already within our intellect when we come into existence. Both of these are similar cases.

But there is yet another concept by which we can understand religious information to be innate. John Calvin did not seem to think that God directly implanted such knowledge within us. Rather, God gave us the disposition to believe in such concepts which then become realized in the light of certain natural experiences—such as seeing the starry firmament on a clear night. Mavrodes concludes that either explanation for the arising of innate knowledge is reasonable, unless one disbelieves in the very existence of God.

The *Manifestation Model* is the second schema that Mavrodes examines (268). Here, we must grasp the distinction between *claiming* that something is the case and *manifesting* this fact. Mavrodes provides the simple example of Bill passing Mary a note claiming that he speaks English, as opposed to actually speaking English before her. Similarly, God may claim his existence through scripture; but he may also *manifest* (reveal) his existence to us by way of some divine *experience*.

But the real question that arises from this model is how we are to ascertain that such a manifestation of God has actually been experienced. What is it about an experience that warrants *that* belief? Mavrodes hypothesizes two plausibilities. First, we may have an experience of God's presence though not be able to articulate it, much as we may sometimes recognize a friend's presence though be unable to satisfactorily explain it. Or, secondly, we may not recognize God's presence at all, but find ourselves intuiting or following a particularly inspired new line of reasoning. Mavrodes considers this to be equally an endowment of God.

The last and best-known model of revelation that Mavrodes offers is the *Communication Model*. Here, he is most concerned to remove any misunderstandings which may arise. For example, some may argue that communicating with humans is beneath the dignity of God. To this Mavrodes responds simply that "'if God in fact speaks to men and women, then . . . so much the worse for any conception of the divine nature with which such speaking is incompatible'" (269). In fact, he jests, God may not limit himself to only speaking theological and religious truths: It is "'a real possibility . . . that God is just not as spiritually minded as are some theologians.'"

Another doubt is that revelation may make it unnecessary for an individual to exercise intellectual initiative. But Mavrodes finds this objection insubstantial. Many individuals do not surrender their autonomy; they reject what God reveals. And those who accept revelation also maintain their autonomy as much as a chemist does not surrender his autonomy merely because he relies on the accuracy of the labels on the bottles of chemicals he utilizes. Similarly, believers do not damage their autonomy because they accept some information which is divinely revealed as part of their overall theology.

Finally, Mavrodes examines the question of revelation as it occurs when we are affected by scriptural narratives or the events in our own lives or in those of others. Should we accept these at face value? Mavrodes argues that there is much to be gained interpretively and inspirationally, and that this higher 'reading' is made possible by an act of the Holy Spirit (270).

Mavrodes ultimately admits that the only satisfying proof that such mediated communication takes place is when we ourselves become a party to it. Though an unbeliever may not be impressed, the unbeliever would still have to admit that Mavrodes has at least clarified many of the important issues, an important step in the philosophical process of inquiry.

We may use Mavrodes's three models as a means to investigate the Vaishnava conception of revelation. The *Causation Model*, in which innate knowledge comes along with birth, is stored in the memory and brought to consciousness later on, could have been borrowed as easily from the Indian sages of antiquity as from Plato's Socratic dialogue. The Vaishnavas hold that we are all originally God conscious, but that our memory of God has been covered due to our contact with matter. Through proper association, our dormant God consciousness or Krishna consciousness can be reawakened, much as Socrates's questions revived the slave boy's memory. If in fact we were originally with God, then those clear impressions of God are stored and need only be revived. Though Calvin made a distinction between direct implantation of an idea of the divine from simply a natural disposition to believe in the divine, Vaishnavas would argue that our prior acquaintance with God means that there is the possibility of a clear recollection of that association rather than merely a disposition to believing in it. Calvin's belief that natural sensations can evoke our God consciousness is fully supported by Vaishnava texts. The entire Tenth Chapter of the *Gita* is wholly devoted to citing numerous examples found in nature which, Krishna tells Arjuna, can activate our memory of the Godhead. Arjuna asks:

> Please tell me in detail of Your divine opulences by which You pervade all these worlds. O Krsna, O supreme mystic, how shall I constantly think of You, and how shall I know You? In what various forms are You to be remembered, O Supreme Personality of Godhead? (10:16-17)

In response, Krishna describes himself in terms of the wonders of nature: "Of bodies of water I am the ocean"; "of immovable things I am the Himalayas"; "of weapons I am the thunderbolt"; "of fishes I am the shark"; "of seasons I am the flower-bearing spring"; "among women I am fame, fortune, fine speech, memory, intelligence, steadfastness and patience"; "I am victory, I am adventure, and I am the strength of the strong."; "of all sciences I am the spiritual science of the self, and among logicians I am the conclusive truth"; "and of secret things I am silence, and of the wise I am the wisdom." Lord Krishna reminds Arjuna that what he has spoken is but a mere indication of his infinite opulences: "Know that all opulent, beautiful, and glorious creations spring from but a spark of My splendor." Krishna's intention is certainly as Calvin has indicated—to point out those excellences of nature that can nourish the human disposition already inclined to worship God.

In discussing the *Manifestion Model*, Mavrodes indicates that we may perceive God's presence indirectly in the subtle form of our unique reasoning ability. The Vaishnavas explain that reason is a function of the intellect, guided by the Lord who is present within each of us as the Supersoul. The following verse from the *Bhagavata Purana* explains that we may perceive the presence of the indwelling Lord through the functioning of the intellect:

> The Personality of Godhead Lord Sri Krsna is in every living being along with the individual soul. And this fact is perceived and hypothesized in our acts of seeing and taking help from the intelligence. (2.2.35)

The Supersoul reveals himself—makes his presence felt—in the working of the intellect. This may not always be recognized, perhaps due to ignorance, or to disbelief in God, etc. But to the believer who is alert to God's presence within, the capacity for right reasoning is seen as a confirmation of God's inner direction. And this is not in itself unreasonable, as Mavrodes says, for we may as much have a spiritual capacity for recognizing God, as we do a physical capacity for recognizing trees.

The Vaishnava would expect such inner direction, for

Krishna asserts in the *Gita* that he directly involves himself in the intellectual process:

> To those who are constantly devoted to serving Me with love, I give the understanding by which they can come to Me. To show them special mercy, I, dwelling in their hearts, destroy with the shining lamp of knowledge the darkness born of ignorance. (10:10-11)

In the commentary to the above verse, Bhaktivedanta Swami Prabhupada explains how revelation lies beyond the range of reason:

> The modern philosophers think that without discriminating one cannot have pure knowledge. For them this answer is given by the Supreme Lord: those who are engaged in pure devotional service, even though they be without sufficient education and even without sufficient knowledge of the Vedic principles, are still helped by the Supreme God, as stated in this verse.
>
> The Lord tells Arjuna that basically there is no possibility of understanding the Supreme Truth, the Absolute Truth, the Supreme Personality of Godhead, simply by speculating, for the Supreme Truth is so great that it is not possible to understand Him or to achieve Him simply by making a mental effort. Man can go on speculating for several millions of years, and if he is not devoted, if he is not a lover of the Supreme Truth, he will never understand Krsna, or the Supreme Truth. Only by devotional service is the Supreme Truth, Krsna, pleased, and by His inconceivable energy He can reveal Himself to the heart of the pure devotee. The pure devotee always has Krsna within his heart; and with the presence of Krsna who is just like the sun, the darkness of ignorance is at once dissipated. This is the special mercy rendered to the pure devotee by Krsna.

What we have here is a manifestation of God working internally, perhaps even unknown to the devotee, to purify the devotee of ignorance. A devotee will come to recognize that the Lord was working within when the devotee finds himself free of the inebrieties that once plagued him.

There are, however, instances in which God can communicate

directly: the *Communication Model.* After all, this is exactly what is supposed to be happening in the Krishna-Arjuna *Gita* dialogue. In response to the argument that it is beneath God's dignity to communicate with humans, we may point out that it is not with just *any* human that he speaks. Moses, for example, was not just *any* mortal. Krishna specified previously that he would provide understanding to those who are *constantly devoted* and who *serve* him with *love.* Again, in the text which opened this discussion cited from the *Svetashvatara Upanishad,* the qualification of *"implicit faith"* in both the Lord and the spiritual master" is necessary before the Vedic knowledge is "automatically revealed." And again, at the outset of the Ninth Chapter of the *Bhagavad-gita,* Krishna tells Arjuna: "My dear Arjuna, because you are never envious of Me, I shall impart to you this most confidential knowledge and realization." It is only with such highly qualified persons that God directly converses. Indeed, such persons are worthy of his eternal association.

Nor can it be said that such divine revelation affects human autonomy. God instructs, but never forces. The element of choice is always available to humans, as we can see in the following final exchange between Krishna and Arjuna:

> Krsna said: O son of Prtha [Arjuna], O conqueror of wealth, have you heard this with an attentive mind? And are your ignorance and illusions dispelled?

> Arjuna said: My dear Krsna, O infallible one, my illusion is now gone. I have regained my memory by Your mercy. I am now firm and free from doubt and am prepared to act according to Your instructions. (18:72-73)

It is interesting to note that Arjuna states that he has *regained* his *memory.* This is again a confirmation of the *Causation Model.* Krishna was acting as Arjuna's spiritual master and it was his duty to inquire from Arjuna whether he had understood the whole *Bhagavad-gita* properly. If not, Krishna was prepared to re-explain any point for Arjuna's clarification.

This concludes our brief comparison of some of the essential doctrines of Christian theology and their Vaishnava equivalents. We would again remind the reader that the citations from contemporary Christian philosophers develop only one idea of each doctrine—the classical (traditional) interpretation. There is certainly a wide range of other possible interpretations for each of these doctrines within the Christian community. Peterson et al. set out some of the possible polarities:

> Views on the Incarnation, for example, range all the way from the traditional claim that Jesus Christ was fully human and fully God to the contention that Jesus was a man who received divine insight to the highest degree humanly possible. Views on scriptural revelation range from the claim that God directly dictated every word to the contention that the Bible at best contains the most illuminating human thought about God to date. And views on the Atonement range all the way from the traditional claim that Christ died to "pay the price for sin" to the claim that Christ's death was a moral example of what divine love can lead one person to do for another. (271)

Nor have these philosophers tried to prove any of these doctrines; they have tried to analyze their meaning and ascertain whether or not they are reasonable. In a like manner, our presentation of the Vaishnava views is by no means exhaustive. A number of differing Vaishnava schools have existed for more than a millennium, each maintaining its own perspective on important matters of doctrine. And, as can be expected, each school also has its many branches. What we have presented herein follows the Brahma-Madhva-Gaudiya Vaishnava school of thought, as articulated by its modern-day exponent A. C. Bhaktivedanta Swami Prabhupada. Our intention has been to demonstrate the interreligious nature of essential Christian doctrines. If there appears to be a surprising sympathy and even agreement with the Vaishnava viewpoint, it is due to their common monotheistic basis.

Works Cited

Beyers, Dan. "Maryland Witnesses Hindu God's Mysterious Thirst for Milk." *Washington Post* 23 Sept. 1995, final ed.: A1.

Bhaktivinode Thakur. *The Bhagavata: Its Philosophy, Its Ethics & Its Theology.* Ed. Shrimad Bhakti Vedanta Baman Maharaj. Nabadwip (Nadia) W.B. India: Shri Devananda Goudiya Math, 1986.

_____. *Shri Chaitanya Shikshamritam.* Trans. Sri Bijoy Krishna Rarhi, M.A. Madras: Sree Gaudiya Math, 1983.

Deadwyler, William. "The Contribution of Bhagavata-Dharma Toward a 'Scientific Religion' and a 'Religious Science.'" *Synthesis of Science and Religion.* Ed. T.D. Singh. Singapore: Palace Press, 1988.

Kundali dasa, ed. *Sri Gaudiya Kanthahara, A Necklace of Vaishnava Verse.* New Delhi: Eye of the Bird Books.

Peterson, Michael et al. *Reason and Religious Belief: An Introduction to the Philosophy of Religion.* New York: Oxford University Press, 1991.

Prabhupada, A.C. Bhaktivedanta Swami. *Bhagavad-Gita As It Is* (2nd Edition). Singapore: Bhaktivedanta Book Trust, 1989.

_____. *Conversations With Srila Prahbupada.* 37 vols. Los Angeles: Bhaktivedanta Book Trust, 1989.

_____. *Dialectic Spiritualism, A Vedic View of Western Philosophy.* Singapore: Prabhupada's Books, 1985.

_____. *Easy Journey to Other Planets.* Los Angeles: Bhaktivedanta Book Trust, 1972.

_____. *Life Comes From Life.* Los Angeles: Bhaktivedanta Book Trust, 1979.

_____. *The Nectar Of Instruction.* Los Angeles: Bhaktivedanta Book Trust, 1975.

_____. *The Science of Self-Realization*. Los Angeles: Bhaktivedanta Book Trust, 1977.

_____. *Sri Chaitanya-charitamrita*. 17 vols. Los Angeles:Bhaktivedanta Book Trust, 1975.

_____. *Srimad-Bhagavatam*. 12 cantos. Singapore: Bhaktivedanta Book Trust, 1987.

Singh, T.D. "Vedantic Views on Evolution." *Synthesis of Science and Religion*. Ed. T.D. Singh. Singapore: Palace Press, 1988.

Suggested Reading[1]

Religious Experiences

Alston, William. "Christian Experience and Christian Belief." Alvin Plantinga and Nicholas Wolterstorff, eds., *Religion and Rationality*, Notre Dame, IN: University of Notre Dame Press, 1983.

James, William. *The Varieties of Religious Experience*. New York: New American Library, 1958.

Katz, Steven T., ed. *Mysticism and Philosophical Analysis*. Oxford: Oxford University Press, 1978.

Proudfoot, Wayne. *Religious Experience*. Berkeley: University of California Press, 1985.

Otto, Rudolf. *The Idea of the Holy*. London: Oxford University Press, 1958.

Stace, W. T. *Mysticism and Philosophy*. New York: Macmillan, 1960.

Swinburne, Richard. *The Existence of God*. London: Oxford University Press, 1979, chap. 13.

Underhill, Evelyn. *Mysticism*. Cleveland, OH: Meridian Books, 1955.

Theistic Arguments

Craig, William L. *The Kalam Cosmological Argument*. New York: Barnes & Noble, 1979.

_____. *The Cosmological Argument from Plato to Leibniz*. New York: Barnes & Noble, 1980.

---

[1] from Peterson et al.

Davis, Stephen T. "What Good are Theistic Proofs?" Louis P. Pojman, ed., *Philosophy of Religion*. Belmont, CA: Wadsworth, 1987, pp. 80-88.

Dore, Clement. *Theism*. Dordrecht, Netherlands: D. Reidel, 1984.

Flew, Antony. *God and Philosophy*. London: Hutchinson, 1966, chaps. 3-5.

Hick, John, and Arthur C. McGill, eds. *The Many Faced Argument*. New York: Macmillan, 1967.

Hume, David. *Dialogues Concerning Natural Religion*. Indianapolis: Hackett, 1980.

Kenny, Anthony. *The Five Ways*. New York: Schocken Books, 1969.

Lewis, C. S. *Mere Christianity*. New York: Macmillan, 1943.

Owen, H. P. *The Moral Argument for Christian Theism*. London: Allen & Unwin, 1965.

Plantinga, Alvin. *God, Freedom and Evil*. New York: Harper & Row, 1974, Part II.

Reichenback, Bruce R. *The Cosmological Argument: A Reassessment*. Springfield, IL: Charles Thomas, 1972.

Rowe, William R. *The Cosmological Argument*. Princeton, NJ: Princeton University Press, 1975.

Swinburne, Richard. *The Existence of God*. Oxford: Clarendon Press, 1979.

Taylor, Richard. *Metaphysics*. Englewood Cliffs, NJ: Prentice Hall, 1983, chap. 7.

Tennant, F. R. *Philosophical Theology* II. Cambridge: Cambridge University Press, 1930.

Yandell, Keith. *Christianity and Philosophy*. Grand Rapids, MI: Eerdmans, 1984, chap. 2.

The Problem of Evil

Griffin, David Ray. *God, Power, and Evil: A Process Theodicy*. Philadelphia: Westminster, 1976.

Hick, John. *Evil and the God of Love.* 1968; reprint and rev. ed., San Francisco: Harper & Row, 1978.

Mackie, J. L. *The Miracle of Theism.* Oxford: Clarendon Press, 1982, chap. 9.

Madden, Edward, and Peter Hare. *Evil and the Concept of God.* Springfield, IL: Charles C. Thomas, 1968.

Peterson, Michael. *Evil and the Christian God.* Grand Rapids, MI: Baker Book House, 1982.

Plantinga, Alvin. *God, Freedom and Evil.* 1974; reprint ed., Grand Rapids, MI: Eerdmans, 1977.

Religious Language: How Can We Speak Meaningfully of God?

Ayer, A. J. *Language, Truth, and Logic.* New York: Dover, 1952.

Ferré, Frederick. *Language, Logic and God.* New York: Harper & Row, 1969.

Gilkey, Langdon. *Naming the Whirlwind.* Indianapolis: Bobbs-Merrill, 1969.

Gibson, Etienne. *Linguistics and Philosophy.* Notre Dame, IN: University of Notre Dame Press, 1988.

High, Dallas, ed. *New Essays in Religion Language.* New York: Oxford University Press, 1969.

Mascall, E. L. *Words and Images.* New York: Ronald Press, 1957.

Ramsey, Ian. *Religious Language.* London: SCM Press, 1957.

_____, ed. *Words about God: The Philosophy of Religion.* New York: Harper & Row, 1971.

Miracles: Does God Intervene in Earthly Affairs?

Ahern, Dennis. "Miracles and Physical Impossibility," *Canadian Journal of Philosophy* 7 (1977): 71-79.

Basinger, David, and Randall Basinger. *Philosophy and Miracle: The Contemporary Debate.* Lewiston, NY: Edwin Mellen Press, 1986.

Brown, Colin. *Miracles and the Critical Mind.* Grand Rapids, MI: Eerdmans, 1983.

Hume, David. *Enquiries Concerning the Human Understanding and Concerning the Principles of Morals,* 2nd ed., L.A. Selby-Bigge, ed. Oxford: Clarendon Press, 1972.

Kellenberger, James. "Miracles," *International Journal for Philosophy of Religion* 10 (1979): 145-62.

Lewis, C. S. *Miracles,* rev. ed. London: Collins, Fontana Books, 1960.

McKinnon, Alistair. "'Miracles' and 'Paradox,'" *American Philosophical Quarterly* 4 (October 1967): 308-14.

Nowell-Smith, Patrick. "Miracles—The Philosophical Approach," *The Hibbert Journal* 48 (1950): 354-60.

Odegard, Douglas. "Miracles and Good Evidence," *Religious Studies* 18 (1982): 37-46.

Walker, Ian. "Miracles and Violations," *International Journal for Philosophy of Religion* 13 (1982): 103-8.

Young, Robert. "Miracles and Epistemology," *Religious Studies* 8 (1972): 115-26.

Life After Death:
Are There Reasons for Hope?

Badham, Paul, and Linda Badham. *Immortality and Extinction?* New York: Barnes and Noble, 1982.

Hick, John. *Death and Eternal Life.* New York: Harper & Row, 1976.

Lewis, H. D. *The Self and Immortality.* New York: Seabury, 1973.

Moody, Raymond A., Jr. *Life After Life.* New York: Bantam Books, 1976.

Penelhum, Terence. *Immortality.* Belmont, CA: Wadsworth, 1973.

_____. *Survival and Disembodied Existence*. London: Routledge & Kegan Paul, 1970.

Perry, John. *Personal Identity and Immortality*. Indianapolis: Hackett, 1979..

Phillips, D. Z. *Death and Immortality*. New York: Macmillan, 1970.

Reichenback, Bruce R. *Is Man the Phoenix? A Study of Immortality*. Grand Rapids, MI: William B. Eerdmans, 1978.

Shoemaker, Sidney, and Richard Swinburne. *Personal Identity*. Oxford: Oxford University Press, 1984.

Swinburne, Richard. *The Evolution of the Soul*. Oxford: Oxford University Press, 1986.

Religion and Science: Compatible or Incompatible?

Barbour, Ian G., ed. *Science and Religion: New Perspectives on the Dialogue*. New York: Harper & Row, 1968.

Davies, Paul. *God and the New Physics*. New York: Simon & Schuster, 1983.

Dillenberger, John. *Protestant Thought and Natural Science*. New York: Doubleday, 1960.

Hawking, Steven. *A Brief History of Time: From Big Bang to Black Holes*. New York: Bantam, 1988.

Nibelsick, Harold. *Theology and Science in Mutual Modification*. New York: Oxford University Press, 1981.

O'Connor, Daniel, and Francis Oakley, eds. *Creation: The Impact of an Idea*. New York: Scribners, 1969.

Mascall, E. L. *Christian Theology and Natural Science*. London: Oxford University Press, 1979.

Polkinghorne, John. *One World*. Princeton, NJ: Princeton University Press, 1987.

_____. *The Way the World Is: The Christian Perspective of a Scientist*. London: Triangle, 1983.

Ratzsch, Del. *Philosophy of Science: The Natural Sciences in Christian Perspective.* Downers Grove, IL: InterVarsity Press, 1986.

Rolston III, Holmes. *Science and Religion: A Critical Examination.* Philadelphia: Temple University Press, 1986.

Schlesinger, George. *Religion and Scientific Method.* Dordrecht, Netherlands: D. Deidel, 1977.

Religious Pluralism:
How Can We Understand Religious Diversity?

Byrne, Peter. "John Hick's Philosophy of World Religions," *Scottish Journal of Theology* 35, no. 4 (1982): 289-301.

Hick, John. *God and the Universe of Faiths.* London: Macmillan, 1977.

Hick, John, advisory ed. *Faith and Philosophy* 5, no. 4 (Oct. 1988).

Hick, John, ed. *Problems of Religious Pluralism.* New York: St. Martin's Press, 1985.

Hick, John, and Brian Hebblethwaite, eds. *Christianity and Other Religions.* Glasgow: Collins, 1980.

Smith, Wilfred Cantwell. *Towards a World Theology.* Philadelphia: Westminster, 1981.

Yandell, Keith E. "Religious Experience and Rational Appraisal," *Religious Studies* 8 (June 1974): 173-87.

Religious Ethics:
The Relation of God to Morality

Donagan, Allan. *The Theory of Morality.* Chicago: University of Chicago Press, 1977.

Frankena, William. *Ethics,* 2nd ed. Englewood Cliffs, NJ: Prentice-Hall, 1973.

Gill, Robin. *A Textbook of Christian Ethics.* Edinburgh: TPT Clark, 1985.

McClendon, James W., Jr. Ethics: *Systematic Theology,* vol. I. Nashville, TN: Abingdon, 1986.

Outka, Gene, and John P. Reeder, Jr., eds. *Religion and Morality.* Garden City, NY: Anchor Boods, 1973.

Quinn, Philip. *Divine Commands and Moral Requirements.* Oxford: Oxford University Press, 1978.

Veatch, Henry. *For an Ontology of Morals.* Evanston, IL: Northwestern University Press, 1971.

Yandell, Keith, ed. *God, Man and Religion: Readings in Philosophy of Religion,* New York: McGraw-Hill, 1973.

Philosophy and Theological Doctrine: Christianity and Vaishnavism in Parallel

Alston, William. "Christian Experience and Christian Belief." Alvin Plantinga and Nicholas Wolterstorff, eds., *Faith and Rationality: Reason and Belief in God.* Notre Dame, IN: University of Notre Dame Press, 1983.

Baillie, John. *The Idea of Revelation in Recent Thought.* New York: Columbia University Press, 1956.

Basinger, David. "Why Petition an Omnipotent, Omniscient, Sholly Good God?" *Religious Studies* 19 (1983): 25-41.

Daujat, Jean. *The Theology of Grace.* Vol. 23 in Henri Daniel-Raps, ed., *Twentieth Century Encyclopedia of Catholicism.* New York: Hawthorne Books, 1959.

Goulder, Michael, ed. *Incarnation and Myth: The Debate Continued.* Grand Rapids, MI: Eerdmans, 1979.

James, William. *The Varieties of Religious Experience.* New York: Modern Library, 1902.

Jantzen, Grace. "Incarnation and Epistemology." *Theology* 83 (May 1983).

Lampe, G. W. H. *God as Spirit.* Oxford: Clarendon Press, 1977.

Morris, Thomas. *The Logic of God Incarnate.* Ithaca, NY: Cornell University Press, 1986.

Quinn, Philip. "Christian Atonement and Kantian Justification," *Faith and Philosophy* 3 (1986): 440-62.

Young, Robert. "Petitioning God," *American Philosophical Quarterly* 11 (1974): 193-201.